A BOOK OF CONDOLENCES

A BOOK OF CONDOLENCES

CLASSIC LETTERS OF BEREAVEMENT

Edited by

Rachel Harding & Mary Dyson

With a Foreword by
Madeleine L'Engle

And a Preface by
Ann Farrer

A Giniger Book
published in association with
CONTINUUM • NEW YORK

1999

The Continuum Publishing Company
370 Lexington Avenue
New York, NY 10017

Published in association with the K. S. Giniger Company, Inc.
250 West 57th Street, New York, NY 10107

Printed in the United States of America

LIBRARY OF CONGRESS CATALOGING IN PUBLICATION DATA

Main entry under title:
A BOOK OF CONDOLENCES

   Includes indexes.
   1. Consolation – Addresses, essays, lectures.
   2. Bereavement – Addresses, essays, lectures.
   I. Harding, Rachel II. Dyson, Mary.

BV4905.2.B65   155.9 37   81 – 5587
ISBN 0-8264-1168-1   AACR2

Grief is crowned with consolation.

SHAKESPEARE, *Antony and Cleopatra* (1606).

CONTENTS

FOREWORD

WHAT IS there to say? When we try to write a letter of condolence to a friend our pen falters; we feel inadequate; perhaps a little embarrassed in the face of death (Byron wrote that he could not understand why he kept laughing); and the right words will not come.

So I turned to this book of letters of condolence, written by great people throughout history, looking for enlightenment. And I discovered that we are all in the same predicament: there is nothing to say except 'I love you, and I care.' Oddly enough (or perhaps it is not odd), the longer the letter, the less adequate the words.

Charlotte Bronte, writing about the death of one of her pupils, speaks for us all when she says, 'Anne Carter, it seems, is *dead*.' We cannot quite believe it. We are shocked, personally outraged.

One of the most comforting letters is George Bernard Shaw's to Mrs Patrick Campbell after her son was killed in action in World War I. 'It's no use,' he says, 'I can't be sympathetic; these things simply make me furious. I want to swear. I *do* swear.' He is angered by words of piousness from a chaplain, and he closes, 'Oh, damn, damn, damn, damn, damn, damn, damn, damn, DAMN.

'And oh, dear, dear, dear, dear, dear, dearest!'

D. H. Lawrence, in writing to John Middleton Murry after Katherine Mansfield's death, writes, '. . . it makes me afraid. As if worse were coming. I feel like the Sicilians. They always cry for help from their dead – we shall have to cry out to ours: we do cry.' And he concludes, 'I wish it needn't have all been as it has been. I do wish it.'

Jessica Mitford cries out, 'Oh, Sister, I was so *desperately* sad to hear . . . what can I say. I know how *terrible* it is for you . . . Sister, this is just to bring you *all* my love.'

Several writers urge the bereaved person to come to them. We sense that an embrace, the clasp of a hand, can say more than all our words. Even for those of us who are believers in the Christian promise, words 'slip and slide.'

But we struggle; we try. Edith Sitwell writes to Wilfred Owen's mother, 'Tomorrow, his first poems in book form will be with you – the immortality of his great soul. What a wonderful moment it will be for you, though an agony, too.

'I cannot write more, because words are so little; before the face of your loss and your grief, they sound too cold.

'I shall write in a few days' time. God bless you.'

T. E. Lawrence, writing to Thomas Hardy's widow, says, 'This is not the letter I'd like to write . . . oh, you will be miserably troubled now, with jackal things that don't matter: you, who have helped so many people, and whom, therefore, no one can help. I am so sorry.'

I am so sorry. Even the great writers stumble into childlike inarticulateness, and that is, in itself, comforting. Even the great writers, in fumbling for words of condolence, are staggered by their own mortality. We reach out toward each other and toward God in a cloud of unknowing.

Even the holy Macarius can say only, 'I thank you for having unveiled to me the sadness of your grief-stricken heart . . . Complete, perfect, detailed compassion is the only answer I can give. . . .'

We search for answers. Father Andrew helps when he writes, 'I don't fear for poor X in the least. I have got very strong positive beliefs, but no negative ones, and I am perfectly certain that God is more beautiful than Religion.'

And C. S. Lewis, writing to Owen Barfield after the death of Charles Williams, says, 'It has been a very odd experience. This, the first really severe loss I have suffered has (a) given a corroboration of my belief in immortality such as I never dreamed of . . . What the idea of death has done to him is nothing to what he has done to the idea of death. . . .'

But Aldous Huxley feels it with questions, as he talks about D. H. Lawrence's 'restatement of the strange Christian doctrine of the resurrection of the body. To his mind, the survival of the spirit was not enough; for the spirit is a man's conscious identity, and Lawrence did not want it to be always identical to himself. He wanted to know otherness – to know it by being it, know it in the flesh, which is always essentially *other*. Therefore there must be a resurrection of the body.' It was difficult for Huxley's rational mind to grasp Lawrence's intuitive mysticism.

'It's a short walk from the womb to the tomb,' remarked the night doorman in our apartment building. In these letters, the writers share what they feel about that walk, their questions, their outrage, their ultimate affirmation. It is good to know that we do not walk alone.

Madeleine L'Engle

PREFACE

Letters of condolence: what a fascinating and unusual subject!

We are thrown at once into a world of deepest feeling: a feeling, however, that can be very difficult to meet. Some people, indeed, entirely fail to meet it and express themselves tritely, falling back, through embarrassment, upon expected, stock formality. A sense of inadequacy, humility, in the face of another person's sorrow, of its being too big for the outsider, who fears to be the fool rushing in, causes them to rely on the safety of platitudes.

Others, possibly because of their own experiences, or perhaps simply through their talent as human beings, write straight from the heart with a love and compassion rarely shown.

Believers and disbelievers, sceptics, agnostics, simple-minded and intellectuals: all are represented in these letters, ranging from 45 BC to the present day.

For those who have known loss and for those who, sadly, will know it, this must be a book of compelling interest.

Rachel Harding and Mary Dyson are to be congratulated on the scope of their research, on the immensity of care that they have taken over sifting and sorting what has come to light, on the imaginative sensitivity in their approach to this material and, above all, on the final presentation of such a tender subject.

Ann Farrer

A BOOK OF CONDOLENCES

EDITORIAL NOTE

We have largely adhered to the original spelling and styling of the letters included in this anthology, but in some of the older letters – where the construction may have appeared to the modern eye as being either ambiguous or obscure, or perhaps even both, we have 'silently' changed whatever we felt was necessary.

A few letters have been shortened by the removal of paragraphs unrelated to the main concern of the letter, and these omissions have not been indicated by typographical leaders as we felt rushing to lines of dots would spoil the appearance of the page and thus hinder the reader's enjoyment.

R.H.   M.D.

LETTER ONE

SERVIUS SULPICIUS RUFUS TO MARCUS TULLIUS
CICERO ON THE DEATH OF CICERO'S DAUGHTER.
ATHENS, MIDDLE OF MARCH 45BC.

I received the news of your daughter's death, with all the concern it so
justly deserves: and indeed I cannot but consider it as a misfortune in
which I bear an equal share with yourself. If I had been near you when
this fatal accident happened, I should not only have mingled my tears
with yours, but assisted you with all the consolation in my power. I am
sensible at the same time, that offices of this kind afford at best but a
wretched relief: for as none are qualified to perform them, but those
who stand near to us by the ties either of blood or affection, such persons
are generally too much afflicted themselves, to be capable of adminis-
tering comfort to others. Nevertheless, I thought proper to suggest a
few reflections, which occurred to me upon this occasion: not as ima-
gining they would be new to you, but believing that in your present
discomposure of mind, they might possibly have escaped your attention. Tell me then, my friend, wherefore do you indulge this excess of
sorrow? Reflect, I entreat you, in what manner fortune has dealt with
every one of us: that she has deprived us of what ought to be no less
dear than our children, and overwhelmed in one general ruin our
honors, our liberties, and our country. And after these losses, is it possible that any other should increase our tears? Is it possible that a mind
long exercised in calamities so truly severe, should not become totally
callous, and indifferent to every event? But you will tell me, perhaps,
that your grief arises not so much on your own account, as on that of
Tullia. Yet surely you must often, as well as my self, have had occasion
in these wretched times to reflect, that their condition by no means
deserves to be regretted, whom death has gently removed from this
unhappy scene. What is there, let me ask, in the present circumstances

of our country, that could have rendered life greatly desirable to your daughter? What pleasing hopes, what agreeable views, what rational satisfaction could she possibly have proposed to her self from a more extended period? Was it in the prospect of conjugal happiness in the society of some distinguished youth? as if, indeed, you could have found a son-in-law amongst our present set of young men, worthy of being entrusted with the care of your daughter! Or was it in the expectation of being the joyful mother of a florishing race, who might possess their patrimony with independence, who might gradually rise thro' the several dignities of the state, and exert the liberty to which they were born in the service and defence of their friends and country? But is there one amongst all these desirable privileges, of which we were not deprived before she was in a capacity of transmitting them to her descendents? Yet after all, you may still allege, perhaps, that the loss of our children is a severe affliction: and unquestionably it would be so, if it were not a much greater to see them live to endure those indignities which their parents suffer.

I lately fell into a reflection, which as it afforded great relief to the disquietude of my own heart, it may possibly contribute likewise to assuage the anguish of yours. In my return out of Asia, as I was sailing from Ægina towards Megara, I amused my self with contemplating the circumjacent countries. Behind me lay Ægina, before me Megara; on my right I saw Piræus, and on my left, Corinth. These cities, once so florishing and magnificent, now presented nothing to my view but a sad spectacle of desolation. 'Alas, (I said to my self) shall such a short-lived creature as man complain, when one of his species falls either by the hand of violence, or by the common course of nature, whilst in this narrow compass so many great and glorious cities, formed for a much longer duration, thus lie extended in ruins? Remember then, oh my heart! the general lot to which man is born: and let that thought suppress thy unreasonable murmurs.' Believe me, I found my mind greatly refreshed and comforted by these reflections. Let me advise you in the same manner to represent to your self, what numbers of our illustrious countrymen have lately been cut off at once, how much the strength of the Roman republic is impaired, and what dreadful devastation has gone forth throughout all its provinces! And can you, with the impression of these greater calamities upon your mind, be so immoderately afflicted for the loss of a single individual, a poor, little, tender woman? who, if she had not died at this time, must in a few fleeting years more have inevitably undergone that common fate to which she was born.

Reasonable however as these reflections are, I would call you from them awhile, in order to lead your thoughts to others more peculiarly suitable to your circumstances and character. Remember then, that your daughter lived as long as life was worth possessing, that is, till liberty was no more: that she lived to see you in the illustrious offices of prætor, consul, and augur; to be married to some of the noblest youths in Rome; to be blessed with almost every valuable enjoyment; and at length to expire with the republic itself. Tell me now, what is there in this view of her fate, that could give either her or your self just reason to complain? In fine, do not forget that you are Cicero; the wise, the philosophical Cicero, who were wont to give advice to others: nor resemble those unskilful empirics, who at the same time that they pretend to be furnished with remedies for other men's disorders, are altogether incapable of finding a cure for their own. On the contrary, apply to your private use, those judicious precepts you have administered to the public. Time necessarily weakens the strongest impressions of sorrow: but it would be a reproach to your character not to anticipate this its certain effect by the force of your own good sense and judgement. If the dead retain any consciousness of what is here transacted, your daughter's affection, I am sure, was such both to you and to all her relations, that she can by no means desire you should abandon your self to this excess of grief. Restrain it then, I conjure you, for her sake, and for the sake of the rest of your family and friends, who lament to see you thus afflicted. Restrain it too, I beseech you, for the sake of your country, that whenever the opportunity shall serve, it may reap the benefit of your counsels and assistance. In short, since such is our fortune that we must necessarily submit to the present system of public affairs, suffer it not to be suspected, that it is not so much the death of your daughter, as the fate of the republic, and the success of our victors that you deplore.

But it would be ill-manners to dwell any longer upon this subject, as I should seem to question the efficacy of your own good sense. I will only add therefore, that as we have often seen you bear prosperity in the noblest manner, and with the highest applause; shew us likewise that you are not too sensible of adversity, but know how to support it with the same advantage to your character. In a word, let it not be said, that fortitude is the single virtue to which my friend is a stranger.

As for what concerns myself, I will send you an account of the state of this province, and of what is transacting in this part of the world, as soon as I shall hear that you are sufficiently composed to receive the information. Farewell.

See the note subjoined to LETTER TWO *below.*

LETTER TWO

MARCUS TULLIUS CICERO'S REPLY TO SERVIUS
SULPICIUS RUFUS.
 ASTURA, 45BC.

I join with you, my dear Sulpicius, in wishing you had been in Rome
when this most severe calamity befell me. I am sensible of the advantage
I should have received from your presence, and your generous, I had
almost said equal participation of my grief, by having found myself
somewhat more compos'd after I had read your letter. It furnished me
indeed with arguments extremely proper to sooth the anguish of affliction; and evidently flowed from a heart that sympathized with the sorrows it endeavoured to assuage. But altho' I could not enjoy the benefit
of your own good offices in person, I had the advantage however of
your son's: who gave me a proof by every tender assistance that could
be contributed upon so melancholy an occasion, how much he imag-
ined he was acting agreeably to your sentiments, when he thus discovered the affection of his own. More pleasing instances of his friendship,
I have frequently received; but never any that were more obliging. As
to those for which I am indebted to your self; it is not only the force of
your reasonings, and I had almost said the equal share you take in my
afflictions, that have contributed to compose my mind; it is the defer-
ence likewise which I always pay to the authority of your sentiments.
For knowing, as I perfectly do, the superior wisdom with which you
are enlightened, I should be ashamed not to support my distresses in the
manner you assure me I ought. I will acknowledge nevertheless, that
they sometimes almost entirely overcome me: and I am scarce able to
resist the force of my grief when I reflect, that I am destitute of those
consolations which attended others, whose examples I propose to my
imitation. Thus Quintus Maximus lost a son of consular rank, and distinguished by many brave and illustrious actions; Lucius Paulus was

deprived of two sons in the space of a single week; and your relation Gallus, together with Marcus Cato, had both of them the unhappiness to survive their respective sons, who were endowed with the highest abilities and virtues. Yet these unfortunate parents lived in times when the honors they derived from the republic might in some measure alleviate the weight of their private sufferings. But as for my self, after having been stripped of those dignities you mention, and which I had acquired by immense labors, I had one only consolation remaining: and of that I am now bereaved! I could no longer divert the disquietude of my thoughts, by employing my self in the causes of my friends, or the business of the state: as I could not with any satisfaction appear either in the forum, or the senate. In short I justly considered my self as cut off from all those occupations in which fortune and industry had qualified me to engage. But I considered too, that this was a deprivation which I suffered in common with your self and some others: and whilst I was endeavouring to break my mind to a patient indurance of those ills; there was *one* to whose tender offices I could have recourse, and in the sweetness of whose conversation I could discharge all the cares and anxiety of my heart. But this last fatal stab to my peace, has torne open those wounds which seemed in some measure to have been tolerably healed. For I can now no longer lose my private sorrows in the prosperity of the commonwealth, as I was wont to dispel the uneasiness I suffered upon the public account, in the happiness I received at home. Accordingly I have equally banished my self from my house, and from the public; as finding no relief in either, from the misfortunes I lament in both. It is this, therefore, that heightens my desire of seeing you here; as nothing can afford me a more effectual consolation than the renewal of our friendly intercourse: a happiness which I hope, and am informed indeed that I shall shortly enjoy. Among the many reasons I have for impatiently wishing your arrival, one is, that we may previously concert together our scheme of conduct in the present conjuncture; which, however, must now be entirely accommodated to another's will. This person, 'tis true, is a man of great abilities and generosity; and one, if I mistake not, who is by no means my enemy; as I am sure he is extremely your friend. Nevertheless it requires much consideration, I do not say in what manner we shall act with respect to public affairs, but by what methods we may best obtain his permission to retire. Farewell.

Marcus Tullius Cicero, 106–43BC, was an orator, statesman, and man of letters. He was a steadfast defender of the Republican cause, but was unsure as to whether he should support Pompey and the aristocracy or Caesar and the new democracy; he finally joined Pompey. Caesar allowed him to live peacefully in retirement and he wrote books on rhetoric and philosophy. After Caesar's death, in his famous Philippics, Cicero stood firm against tyranny and was eventually forced to flee from Rome, but he was captured by bounty hunters and murdered.

Tullia, born in 76BC, was married three times – her third husband being Dolabella, a profligate who alternately supported Caesar and Brutus; he divorced Tullia and she died in childbirth in 45BC.

Servius Sulpicius Rufus, 105–43BC, was a famous jurist. He was consul in 51BC and joined Caesar in the Civil War.

Q. Fabius Maximus Cunctator's son was consul with Tiberius Sempronius Gracchus in 213BC.

L. Paulus defeated Perseus at Pydna in 168BC and lost his sons at the time of his Triumph.

C. Sulpicius Gallus served with Paullus against Perseus and was consul in 166BC. M. Cato, surnamed Censor because of his strict reforms when Censor, lost his son who was praetor designate in 153BC.

From Cicero: Letters to Friends, translated by William Melmoth, London, 1753.

LETTER THREE

FROM THE YOUNGER PLINY TO COLONUS ON THE
DEATH OF POMPEIUS QUINCTIANUS.
  C. AD104.

I greatly admire the generous grief you express for the death of Pompeius Quinctianus, as it is a proof that your affection for your departed
friend, does not terminate with his life. Far different from those who
love, or rather, I should more properly say, who counterfeit love to
none but the living. Nor indeed even *that* any longer than they are the
favourites of fortune; for the unhappy are no more the object of their
remembrance, than the dead. But *your* friendship is raised upon a more
lasting foundation, and the constancy of your affection can only end
with your life. Quinctianus, most certainly, well deserved to meet with
that generous warmth from his friends, of which he was himself so
bright an example. He loved them in prosperity; protected them in
adversity; lamented them in death. How open was his countenance!
how modest his conversation! how equally did he temper gravity with
gaiety! how fond was he of learning! how judicious his sentiments!
how dutiful to a father of a very different character! and how happily
did he reconcile filial piety to inflexible virtue, continuing a good son,
without forfeiting the title of a good man! – But why do I aggravate
your affliction by reminding you of his merit? – yet I know your affection for the memory of this excellent youth is so strong, that you had
rather endure that pain, than suffer his virtues to be passed over in silence;
especially by me, whose applause, you imagine, will adorn his actions,
extend his fame, and restore him, as it were, to that life from which he is
prematurely snatched. Farewell.

See the note for LETTER FOUR.

LETTER FOUR

FROM THE YOUNGER PLINY TO AEFULANUS MAR-
CELLINUS ON THE DEATH OF THEIR FRIEND
FUNDANUS' DAUGHTER.
  C. AD104.

I write to you, impressed with the deepest sorrow: the youngest daughter of my intimate friend Fundanus is dead! Never surely was there a
more agreeable and more amiable young person, or one who better
deserved to have enjoyed a long, I had almost said, an immortal life!
She was scarcely fourteen, and yet united the wisdom of age and dis-
cretion of a matron, with the sprightliness of youth, and sweetness of
virgin modesty. With what an endearing fondness did she hang on her
father's neck! How kindly and respectfully behave to us his friends!
How affectionately treat all those who, in their respective offices, had
the care of her education! She employed much of her time in study and
reading; indulged herself in few diversions, and entered even into those
with singular caution and reserve. With what forbearance, with what
patience, with what fortitude did she endure her last illness! She com-
plied with all the directions of her physicians; encouraged the hopes of
her sister, and her father; and when her strength was totally exhausted,
supported her spirits by the sole force of her own mind. The vigour of
her mind indeed, continued even to her last moments, unbroken by the
pain of a long illness, or the terrors of approaching death: a reflection
which renders the loss of her so much the more sensibly to be lamented
by us. It is a loss infinitely indeed severe! and aggravated by the particular conjuncture in which it happened! She was contracted to a most
worthy youth; the wedding day was fixed, and we were all invited.
How sad a change from the highest joy, to the deepest sorrow! How
shall I express the wound that pierced my heart, when I heard Fundanus
himself (as grief is ever fond of dwelling upon every circumstance to

increase the affliction) ordering the money he had designed to lay out upon clothes and jewels for her marriage, to be employed in myrrh and spices for her funeral? He is a man of great good sense and accomplishments, having applied himself, from his earliest youth, to the noblest arts and sciences; but all the maxims of fortitude and philosophy which he has derived from books, or delivered by his own precepts, he now absolutely rejects; and every firmer virtue of his heart gives place to paternal tenderness. You will excuse, you will even approve his grief, when you consider what a loss he has sustained! He has lost a daughter who resembled him in his manners, as well as his person, and exactly copied out all her father. If you should think proper to write to him upon the subject of a calamity so justly to be deplored, let me remind you not to urge severer arguments of consolation, which seem to carry a sort of reproof with them, but to use those only of a gentle and sympathizing humanity. Time will render him more open to the dictates of reason: for, as a recent wound skrinks from the hand of the surgeon, but gradually submits to, and even requires the means of cure; so a mind under the first impression of a misfortune shuns and rejects all the persuasions of reason, but at length, if applied with tenderness, calmly and willingly resigns itself to consolation. Farewell.

Pliny the Younger – Gaius Plinius Caecilius Secundus, AD62–104. Born at Novum Comum. He was educated at home with tutors and then finished his education in Rome. Here he came into closer contact with his uncle, the Elder Pliny who died during the eruption of Vesuvius; Pliny and his mother were then staying at Misenum where the uncle was in command of the fleet. Pliny the Younger served as tribune, quaestor, praetor and consul. His letters reveal him as a lovable man.

Most well known are the letters written to the Emperor Trajan and those from Trajan in reply, with regard to the treatment of the Christians in Bithynia, which lay along the South coast of the Black Sea; and his eye-witness account of the eruption of Vesuvius, in which his uncle died in AD79.
From Pliny: Letters, *translated by William Melmoth, 1796.*

LETTER FIVE

MARSILIO FICINO TO GISMONDO DELLA STUFA.
FLORENCE, 1 AUGUST 1473.

If each of us, essentially, is that which is greatest within us, which always remains the same and by which we understand ourselves, then certainly the soul is the man himself, and the body is but his shadow. Whatever wretch is so deluded as to think that the shadow of man is man, like Narcissus is dissolved into tears. You will only cease to weep, Gismondo, when you cease looking for your Albiera degli Albizzi in her dark shadow and begin to follow her by her own clear light. For the further she is from the mis-shapen shadow the more beautiful will you find her, past all you have ever known.

Withdraw into your soul, I beg you, where you will possess her soul which is so beautiful and dear to you; or rather, from your soul withdraw to God. There you will contemplate the beautiful idea through which the Divine Creator fashioned your Albiera; and as she is far more lovely in her Creator's form than in her own, so you will embrace her there with far more joy.

Farewell.

Marsilio Ficino (1433–99), born in Florence, received the usual education of the time in Latin, Philosophy and Medicine. He started Greek in 1456 and finally translated the whole of Plato.

Cosimo de Medici gave him the use of a villa in which to study manuscripts, and from here he founded the Platonic Academy, which became one of the chief intellectual centres of Europe.

Ficino was ordained in 1473 and in 1477 wrote De Christiana Religione. *He became the leader of the Platonic Academy and tried to revive Platonism. He had been led to Plato through the writings of Augustine. He thought that philosophy and religion were parallel paths to truth, and so true religion*

(*Christianity*) *and true philosophy* (*Platonism*) *must agree in the end; they both come into being from the contemplation of God. Man's aim should be the contemplation of union with God. Since this can rarely occur in this life, a belief in personal immortality must be postulated. A Platonic friendship is a communion between friends based ultimately on the soul's love for God.*

Ficino uses Ovid's story of Narcissus falling in love with his own reflection, and elaborates it in his De Amore *to suggest that Narcissus, the soul of man, is so seduced by bodily beauty, which is only its shadow reflected in water, that it deserts its own body and so dies.*

From The Ficino Letters, *Volume One – edited and translated by the Language Department of the London School of Economics, London.*

LETTER SIX

FROM ELIZABETH I TO JAMES VI OF SCOTLAND ON
THE DEATH OF HIS MOTHER, MARY QUEEN OF
SCOTS.
14 FEBRUARY 1587.

My dear brother,
I would you knew (though not felt) the extreme dolour that overwhelms
my mind, for that miserable accident which (far contrary to my meaning) hath befallen. I have now sent this kinsman of mine, whom by now
it has pleased you to favour, to instruct you truly of that which is too
irksome for my pen to tell you. I beseech you, as God and many more
know, how innocent I am in this case; so you will believe me, that if I
had bid ought I would have bid by it. I am not so base-minded that
fear of any living creature or prince should make me afraid to do that
were just; or done, to deny the same. I am not of so base a lineage, nor
carry so vile a mind. But, as not to disguise fits not a king, so will I never
dissemble my actions, but cause them show even as I meant them. Thus
assuring yourself of me, that as I know this was deserved, yet if I had
meant it I would never lay it on others' shoulder; no more will I not
damnify myself that thought it not. The circumstance it may please
you to have of this bearer. And for your part, think you have not in the
world a more loving kinswoman, nor a more dear friend than myself;
nor any that will watch more carefully to preserve you and your estate.
And who shall otherwise persuade you, judge them more partial to
others than you. And thus in haste I leave to trouble you: beseeching
God to send you a long reign.
    Your most assured loving sister and cousin
    Eliz. R.

*Queen Elizabeth I, 1533–1603, Queen of England and Ireland from 1558–
1603.*

This letter to James was an attempt on the part of Elizabeth to disassociate herself from the execution of his Mother, Mary Queen of Scots. Having signed the death warrant she later signed a pardon which arrived too late, possibly by design.

James VI of Scotland was said to have received the news of his mother's death with satisfaction – it put him in direct line for the throne of England. On the death of Elizabeth I he ascended the throne and became James I of England. A century later the two crowns – England and Scotland – were united.

From A Treasury of the World's Great Letters, *London, 1941.*

LETTER SEVEN

FROM JOHN DONNE TO SIR HENRY GOODYER ON
THE DEATH OF GOODYER'S WIFE.
PYRFORD, 1604.

Sir,
I live so far removed that even the ill news of your great loss (which is
ever swiftest and loudest) found me not till now. Your letter speaks it
not plain enough; but I am so accustomed to the worst, that I am sure
it is so in this. I am almost glad that I knew her so little, for I would have
no more additions to sorrow. If I should comfort you, it were an alms
acceptable in no other title than when poor give to poor, for I am more
needy of it than you. And I know you well provided of Christian and
learned and brave defences against all human accident. I will make my
best haste after your messenger; and if myself and the place had not
been ill-provided of horses, I had been the messenger, for you have
taught me by granting more to deny no request – Your honest unprofitable friend.
    J. Donne
Pyrford 3 o'clock just as yours came.

See the note following LETTER EIGHT.

LETTER EIGHT

JOHN DONNE TO HIS MOTHER ON THE DEATH OF
HIS SISTER, ANNE. JOHN WAS NOW THE ONLY
SURVIVING CHILD.
1616.

My most dear Mother,
When I consider so much of your life as can fall within my memory
and observations, I find it to have been a sea, under a continual tempest,
where one wave hath ever overtaken another. Our most wise and blessed Saviour chooseth what way it pleaseth Him to conduct those which
He loves to His haven and eternal rest. The way which He hath chosen
for you is strait, stormy, obscure and full of sad apparitions of death and
wants, and sundry discomforts; and it has pleased Him that one dis-
comfort should still succeed and touch another, that He might leave you
no leisure, by any pleasure or abundance to stay or step out of that way,
or almost take breath in that way, by which He hath determined to
bring you home, which is His glorious Kingdom.

I hope therefore, my most dear Mother, that your experience of the
calamities of this life, your continual acquaintance with the visitations
of the Holy Ghost, which gives better inward comforts than the world
can outer discomforts, your wisdom to distinguish the value of this
world from the next, and your religious fear of offending our merciful
God by repining at anything which He doeth, will preserve you from
any inordinate and dangerous sorrow for the loss of my most beloved
sister. For my part, which am only left now to do the office of a child,
though the poorness of my fortune, and the greatness of my charge,
hath not suffered me to express my duty towards you as became me;
yet I protest to you before Almighty God and His Angels and Saints in
Heaven, that I do, and ever shall, esteem myself to be as strongly bound
to look to you and provide for you relief, as for my own poor wife and
children.

'I would have no more additions to sorrow' says Donne. Certainly, his career viewed from the year of 1604, must have seemed one of disappointment and frustration, if nothing worse. His father was a prosperous London ironmonger. Through his mother he was well connected, being related to Sir Thomas More. He was brought up a Catholic, went down from Oxford without a degree, travelled, and in 1592 was admitted to Lincolns Inn. He became an Anglican, accompanied Essex on his Cadiz Expedition and was later appointed Secretary to the Lord Keeper, Sir Thomas Egerton. Here he met many of the chief men of the day and wrote much of his poetry. But, witty, charming and handsome as he was, his marriage to Anne, niece of Sir Thomas Egerton was not approved of and he was dismissed from his post, and for a time committed to prison. Only after an intensive study of theology and ordination in 1615 did his circumstances improve, and then rapidly. By the year 1616 he was a Royal Chaplain and in 1621 he became Dean of St. Paul's. He is generally regarded as the greatest of the 'metaphysical' poets and one of the most impressive Anglican preachers. It is interesting that one of his prose writings supported the view that 'Selfe – Homicide is not so Naturally Sinne that it may never be otherwise'.

From: Letters to Several Persons of Honour, edited by R. Marriot, London, 1651 – LETTER SEVEN. The Life and Letters of Donne, edited by Sir Edmund Gosse, London, 1899 – LETTER EIGHT.

LETTER NINE

ISAAC PENINGTON TO A FRIEND IN LONDON; SUP-
POSED TO BE WRITTEN ON THE OCCASION OF THE
PLAGUE.
8 JULY 1665.

Ah Friend!

Dreadful is the Lord; it is known and felt, beyond what can be spoken.
Doth thy heart fear before him? Art thou willing to be subject to him?
Dost thou desire strength from him? O that thou mayest be helped daily
to cry unto him, that he may have mercy upon thee, who is tender-
hearted and able to preserve, when his arrows fly around about!

Retire, deeply retire, and wait to feel his life; that thy soul may be
gathered out of the reasonings and thoughts of thy mind, into that which
stays from them, and fixes beneath them; where the Lord is known and
worshipped, in that which is of himself, of his own begetting of his own
forming, of his own preserving, of his own shutting and opening at his
pleasure. And, living in the sense and the pure fear of the Lord, (not
meddling to judge others or justify thyself, but waiting for his appearance in thee, who is the justified, and justification), thou wilt be enabled
by the Lord, in his seasons, to bring thy children and family into the
same sense; that thou and they together may enjoy the same preserva-
tion from him, as far as he sees meet, whose will is not to be limited, but
to be subjected to.

And, if thy heart be right before the Lord, and thy soul awakened
and preserved in his fear, thou wilt find somewhat to travel out of, and
somewhat to travel into, and the Lord drawing and leading thee. And
this stroke, which is so dreadful to others, nor altogether without dread
to thee, will prove of great advantage in thy behalf; in drawing thee
more into a sense of acquaintance of the infinite One, and in drawing

thee more from thy earthly thoughts and knowledge, which will not now stand thee instead.

Thy Friend,
I.P.

Isaac Penington, 1616–79, was a Quaker and a close relation of William Penn, and like so many Friends of his day he was noted for the fortitude with which he suffered persecution.

From A transcript of selections from the John Penington MSS., *made by or for John Kendall of Colchester, c.1780.*

LETTER TEN

EXTRACT FROM A LETTER FROM MADAME DE
SÉVIGNÉ TO THE COMTE DE BUSSY-RABUTIN ON
THE DEATH OF TURENNE, MARSHAL OF FRANCE.
FROM PARIS, 6 AUGUST 1675.

You are a very good almanac; like an expert you forecast everything
which happened on the German front; but you did not foresee M. de
Turenne's death, nor the chance cannon shot which picked him out
from among ten or twelve others. For my part, I who see providence at
work in everything, can see this cannon loaded since the dawn of time.
I can see that everything was leading M. de Turenne on towards it, and
I can find nothing baleful in the event, always supposing his conscience
to have been clear.

What did he lack? He died in a blaze of glory. His reputation could
not have been greater; at that very moment he was enjoying the satisfaction of seeing the enemy retreating and was witnessing the fruit of
his labours of the past three months. Sometimes, through the very fact
of living on, one's star burns less brightly. It is safer to have done abrupt-
ly, above all in the case of heroes whose every action is so keenly ob-
served. If the Comte d'Harcourt had died after the capture of the Sainte
Marguerite islands or the relief of Casal, and the Maréchal du Plessis
Praslin after the battle of Rhethel, would not they have been more
renowned? M. de Turenne did not suffer in his death; again, does that
count for nothing?

You are aware of the general sorrow over this loss and the eight new
marshals of France.

*Madame de Sévigné (1626–96) was born in Paris of an ancient Burgundian
family; both her parents died when she was still an infant and she was brought
up by the Abbé de Coulanges, her maternal uncle. She received a good educa-*

tion and at eighteen married the Marquis Henri de Sévigné a spendthrift and a libertine; they had a son and a daughter. Her husband was killed in a duel by a rival in a sordid intrigue. Madame de Sévigné was only 25, brilliantly beautiful and fascinating, but she was unmoved by the flattery of the most dazzling court in the world. Turenne and her cousin de Bussy-Rabutin and others all sought her hand in vain. Her heart was devoted to her children and it is mainly due to the separation from her daughter on the latter's marriage in 1669 that we owe her famous letters.

Roger Comte de Bussy-Rabutin was a courtier and soldier and writer.

Vicomte D'Henri de Latour D'Auvergne Turenne, second son of the Duke of Bouillin and Elizabeth of Nassau, William the silent's daughter, was born at Sedan in 1611. He fought with distinction in the Thirty Years War, was made Marshal of France in 1644, was superseded by Condé but restored; and after many successful campaigns was made Marshal-general in 1660. He was triumphant in Holland, ravaged the Palatinate, laid waste Alsace, and advanced into Germany. Here he was killed reconnoitering at Sasbach in July 1675.

The Comte D'Harcourt was a great general under Louis XIII who defeated the Spaniards in 1637.

From Les Lettres de Madame Sévigné, Paris. Translated by Mrs Hamilton-Jones.

LETTER ELEVEN

FROM WILLIAM PENN TO MARGARET FOX ON THE
DAY THAT HER HUSBAND GEORGE DIED.
13 JANUARY 1691.

Dear Margaret Fox,
With the dear remembrance of my unfeigned love in Xt Jesus, I am to
be the teller to thee of sorrowful tidings as I may call it in some sense,
which is this, that thy dear husband and my beloved friend, G. Fox, has
finished his glorious testimony this night about half an hour after nine,
being sensible to the last breath.

Oh, he is gone, and has left us in the storm that is over our heads,
surely in great mercy to him, but as an evidence to us of sorrows to
come. He was as living and firm Fourth Day last, was a week at Grace-
church Street, and this last First Day, being the day before yesterday,
but complained after Meeting of being inwardly struck, and lay ever
since at Henry Goldney's where he departed.

My soul is deeply affected with this hasty great loss. Surely it por-
tends to us great evils to come. A Prince indeed is fallen in Israel today.

I cannot enlarge for I shall write to several tonight and it is late. The
Lord be with thee and thine, and us all. Amen.

I am thy faithful and affectionate Friend.

Wm. Penn.

*William Penn (1644-1718), the founder of Pennsylvania, was a follower of
George Fox. Penn was a loyal and splendid Quaker and while in prison wrote
one of his most popular books,* No Cross, No Crown.

*Penn's well known lines are: 'They that love beyond the world cannot be
separated by it. Death cannot kill what never dies. Nor can spirits ever be
divided that love and live in the same Divine Principle; the root and record of
their friendship. If absence be not death, neither is theirs. Death is but crossing*

the world, as friends do the seas; they live in one another still.' And to this day they are often quoted in letters of condolence.

George Fox (1624–90) was the founder of the Society of Friends, and the sad truth about Fox today is that even his own sect, the Society of Friends (Quakers), tend to forget him. His Journal is seldom read, and his admirable Peace Testimony frequently ignored.

George Fox was a great believer in shaking people up. This he called 'being valiant for truth'. Once having arrived at the conviction that God was on his side there was no stopping him. Heroically, ceaselessly and sometimes effectively he and his gallant followers attacked the evils of their day. Impervious to suffering they went in and out of gaol gladly for any cause that they believed to be right.

George Fox wanted people to 'walk cheerfully over the world answering that of God in everyone'.

From The Journal of George Fox, London, 1926.

LETTER TWELVE

EXTRACT FROM A LETTER FROM ALEXANDER
POPE TO HIS FRIEND EDWARD BLOUNT IN
SYMPATHY FOR THE UNSUCCESSFUL REBELLION
OF 1715.
  20 MARCH 1715–6.

Dear Sir,
I find that a real concern is not only a hindrance to speaking, but to
writing too; the more time we give ourselves to think over one's own,
or a Friend's unhappiness, the more unable we grow to express the
grief that proceeds from it. It is as natural to delay a letter, at such a
Season as this, as to retard a melancholy visit to a person one cannot
relieve. One is ashamed in that circumstance, to pretend to entertain
people with trifling, insignificant affectations of sorrow on the one hand,
or unseasonable and forced gayeties on the other. Tis a kind of profana-
tion of things sacred to treat so solemn a matter as a generous voluntary
suffering, with Compliments of Heroic Gallantries. Such a man as I
know you are has no need of being spirited up into honour, or like a
weak woman, praised into an opinion of his own virtue. Tis enough to
do and suffer what we ought; and men should know, that the noble
power of suffering bravely is as far above that of enterprising greatly, as
an unblemished conscience and inflexible resolution are above an acci-
dental Flow of Spirits, or a sudden tide of blood.

See LETTER FIFTEEN.

LETTER THIRTEEN

ALEXANDER POPE TO DR SWIFT ON THE DEATH
OF THEIR FRIEND JOHN GAY
5 DECEMBER 1732.

It is not a time to complain that you have not answered my two letters
(in the last of which I was impatient under some fears). It is not now
indeed a time to think of myself, when one of the nearest and longest
ties I have ever had, is broken all of a sudden, by the unexpected death
of Mr Gay. Good God! How often are we to die before we go quite
off this stage?

In every friend we lose a part of ourselves, and the best part. God
keep those we have left! few are worth praying for, and one's self the
least of all.

I shall never see you now, I believe, one of your principal calls to
England is at an end. Indeed he was the most amiable by far; his qualities were the gentlest; but I love you as well and as firmly. Would to
God the man we have lost had not been so amiable, nor so good! but
that is a wish for our own sakes, not for his. Sure, if innocence and
integrity can deserve happiness, it must be his. Adieu; I can add nothing
to what you will feel, and diminish nothing from it. Yet write to me
and soon. Believe no man now living loves you better; I believe no
man ever did that.

A. Pope.

See LETTER FIFTEEN

LETTER FOURTEEN

FROM DR SWIFT TO ALEXANDER POPE ON THE
DEATH OF POPE'S MOTHER.
   FROM DUBLIN, 8 JULY 1733.

I must condole with you for the loss of Mrs Pope, of whose death the
papers have been full. But I would rather rejoice with you; because, if
any circumstances can make the death of a dear parent and friend a
subject of joy, you have them all. She died in an extreme old age without pain, under the care of the most dutiful son, that I have ever known
or heard of; which is a felicity not happening to one in a million.

See LETTER FIFTEEN.

LETTER FIFTEEN

FROM DR SWIFT TO ALEXANDER POPE ON THE
DEATH OF JOHN GAY.
DUBLIN, 1733.

I received yours with a few lines from the Doctor, and the account of
our losing Mr. Gay, upon which event I shall say nothing. I am only
concerned that long living hath not hardened me. For even in this
Kingdom and in a few days past, two persons of great merit, whom I
loved very well, have died in the prime of their years, but a little above
thirty. I would endeavour to comfort myself upon the loss of friends, as
I do upon the loss of money; by turning to my account book, and
seeing whether I have enough left for my support; but in the former
case I find I have not, any more than in the other; and I know not any
man who is in a greater likelihood than myself to die poor and friendless.
You are a much greater loser than me by his death, as being a more intimate friend, and often his companion; which latter I could never hope
to be, except perhaps once more in my life for a piece of a summer. I
hope he hath left you the care of any writings he may have left, and I
wish, that with those already extant, they could be all published in a
fair edition under your inspection.

*Alexander Pope (1688–1744) was born in London, son of a linen-draper; after
an unmethodical education he quickly gained fame as a poet, wit and satirist
and became a friend of Addison and Steele. His* Essay on Criticism *placed him
in the front rank of men of letters of his day.*

*John Gay (1688–1732), born at Barnstable, was apprenticed to a London
silk mercer but soon took to letters for a livelihood. His most famous work was*
The Beggar's Opera, *the outcome of a suggestion made by Swift in 1716.*

*Jonathan Swift (1667–1745), greatest of English prose satirists came from
Yorkshire and Leicestershire stock, but was born and educated in Dublin. For a*

short time he was secretary to Sir William Temple, but returned to Dublin and took orders. He did not relish country life and so returned to Sir William where he stayed until the latter's death in 1699. Subsequently he divided his time between Dublin and London engaged in political work. After the accession of King George, Swift returned to the Deanery of St Patrick's and except for two journeys to England in 1726 and 1727 remained there for the rest of his life. His voluminous correspondence with Gay, Pope and others records his life during these years.

These three men were joined together in a remarkable literary association – the Scriblerus Club – they scribbled verses and talked nonsense together. Swift saw very little of Pope – hardly knew him until the end of 1713 and they parted in the summer of 1714 and never met again except during Swift's two visits to England in 1726–7.

From their letters however it is clear that they were fond of each other. Gay, Johnson says, was the general favourite of the wits, and Pope was apparently fonder of him than anyone.

In these letters we see a softer side of the satirists, a side not so often revealed in their well known works.

Mrs Pope died 7 June 1733, aged 93.

Edward Blount was a friend of Pope.

From The Correspondence of Alexander Pope, edited by George Sherburn, Oxford, 1956 – LETTERS TWELVE and THIRTEEN. The Correspondence of Swift, edited by Harold Williams, Oxford, 1965 – LETTERS FOURTEEN and FIFTEEN.

LETTER SIXTEEN

ELIZABETH PUREFOY TO THOMAS ROBOTHAM ON
THE DEATH OF HIS WIFE.
FROM SHALSTONE, 9 NOVEMBER 1745.

I received Mr. Robotham's letter of the 1st instant with the sorrowful account of Mrs. Robotham's death; you have lost a very good one, and I believe all her acquaintance may say the same. If sorrow would bring her again I believe we should soon have her amongst us; but as that can't be we must go to her and in the meantime reconcile ourselves as well as we can to our loss of her. We received your kind present of sack and fish for which we return you thanks, they were all exceedingly good. Since I wrote to you last I have sent you three hares with this, which I desire you to accept.

If your health is no better than usual I fear you will not be able to go on with your business, except Nelly can be capable of assisting you. We thank you for your kind proffers of service and all other favours, and send you the measure you desire. Our service and best wishes attend yourself and Nelly and I am.

> Your humble servant
> E.P.

In 1618 Alan Aetes was Lord of the Manor of Shalstone in N. Bucks. His daughter married William Purefoy. Elizabeth Purefoy was born in 1672, was widowed in 1704 and lived a further sixty-one years, managing the estate and garden and running the house with her son, Henry. In the words of her epitaph written by her son and inscribed on the monument to her in Shalstone church: 'She was a woman of excellent understanding, prudent and frugal as well as a true friend to the family she married into.' She was a lady of character, capable and efficent, with little sentiment, as her letters of condolence show. Thomas Robotham, an innkeeper in Islington, was her principal agent, married to an old servant of Elizabeth Purefoy's family. His inn, The King's Head, is mentioned by Mr Pepys several times. There was a considerable exchange of presents between Islington and Shalstone, but there is no evidence that Mr Robotham was paid for his services, although money was sent regularly to him for purchases of fish, coffee, tea, chocolate, fruit, cloth and lace, and watch repairs, together with dairy produce and game from Shalstone. When he died he owed a small sum of money to the Purefoys and his niece by marriage was asked to pay this back.

From The Purefoy Letters 1735–53, edited by G. Eland, London, 1931.

LETTER SEVENTEEN

LADY MARY WORTLEY MONTAGU TO THE
COUNTESS OF BUTE ON THE DEATH OF HER
HUSBAND.
FROM LOUVERE, 20 AUGUST 1752.

My dear Child,
'Tis impossible to tell you to what degree I share with you in the
misfortune that has happened. I do not doubt your own reason will
suggest to you all the alleviations that can serve on so sad an occasion,
and will not trouble you with the common place topics that are used,
generally to no purpose, in letters of consolation. Disappointment ought
to be less sensibly felt at my age than yours; yet I own I am so far affected by this, that I have need of all my philosophy to support it. However, let me beg of you not to indulge in useless grief, to the prejudice
of your health, which is so necessary to your family. Everything may
turn out better than you expect. We see so darkly into futurity, we
never know when we have real cause to rejoice or lament. The worst
appearances have often happy consequences, as the best lead many times
into the greatest misfortunes. Human prudence is very straightly bound-
ed. What is most in our power, though little so, is the disposition of our
own minds. Do not give way to melancholy; seek amusements; be
willing to be diverted, and insensibly you will become so. Weak people
only place a merit in affliction. A grateful remembrance, and whatever
honour we can pay to their memory is all that is owing to the dead.
Tears and sorrow are no duties to them, and make us incapable of those
we owe to the living.
   I give you thanks for your care of my books. I yet retain, and carefully cherish, my taste for reading. If relays of eyes were to be hired like

posthorses I would never admit any but silent companions; they afford a constant variety of entertainment, which is almost the only one pleasing in the enjoyment, and inoffensive in the consequences. I am sorry your sight will not permit you a great use of it. My dear child, endeavour to raise your spirits, and believe this advice comes from the tenderness of your most affectionate mother.

M. Wortley

Lady Mary Wortley Montagu, 1689–1762, letter-writer and poet. Lady Mary Pierrepont was one of the most cultured women of her time and after her marriage in 1712 to Edward Wortley Montagu, grandson of the Earl of Sandwich, moved in aristocratic circles in London renowned for her wit and her beauty. In 1739 she retired to Louvere in Italy, for health reasons, where she enjoyed life in the country and books took the place of society. Her letters from there show how close to her heart was the well being of her daughter, the Countess of Bute, and her grandchildren.

From English Letters of the XVIII Century, *edited by James Aitken, London, 1946.*

LETTER EIGHTEEN

BENJAMIN FRANKLIN TO MISS E. HUBBARD,
DAUGHTER BY ANOTHER MARRIAGE OF THE
SECOND WIFE OF JOHN FRANKLIN.
  FROM PHILADELPHIA, 23 FEBRUARY 1756.

I condole with you. We have lost a dear and valuable relation. But it is the will of God and nature, that these mortal bodies be laid aside, when the soul is to enter into real life. This is a rather embryo estate, a preparation for living.

A man is not completely born until he is dead. Why then should we grieve that a new child is born among the immortals, a new member is added to their happy society? We are spirits. That bodies should be lent us, while they can afford us pleasure, assist us in acquiring knowledge, or in doing good to our fellow creatures, is a kind and benevolent act of God. When they become unfit for these purposes, and afford us pain instead of pleasure, instead of an aid become an encumbrance, and answer none of the intentions for which they were given, it is equally kind and benevolent that a way is provided by which we may get rid of them. Death is that way. We ourselves, in some cases, prudently choose a partial death. A mangled painful limb which cannot be restored we willingly cut off. He who plucks out a tooth, parts with it freely, since then pain goes with it, and he who quits the whole body, parts at once with all pains and possibilities of pains and diseases which it was liable to or capable of making him suffer.

Our friend and we were invited abroad on a party of pleasure, which is to last for ever. His chair was ready first, and he is gone before us. We could not all conveniently start together; and why should you and I be grieved at this, since we are soon to follow, and know where to find him.

Adieu.

B.F.

Benjamin was born in Boston, Massachusetts, and was apprenticed when he was twelve years old to his brother James, a printer. He later worked in Philadelphia and London, and returned to Philadelphia and established his own printing house, bought the Philadelphia Gazette, and became a journalist. In 1746 he researched electricity and became a F.R.S. In 1757 he was sent to England to insist that Pennsylvania had the right to tax the proprietors of land held under the Penn Charter for the cost of defending it from Frenchmen and Indians. He was successful, and received honorary degrees from Oxford and Edinburgh. In 1764 he again went to England to uphold the right of no taxation without representation: his negotiations failed, and he came back to America and helped to produce the Declaration of Independence. He was sent to Paris in 1776 to get help in the war. He was US Minister in Paris, and on returning home in 1785 was elected President of Philadelphia.

He was a prodigious letter writer.

From A Treasury of the World's Great Letters, London, 1941.

LETTER NINETEEN

DR JOHNSON TO HIS SCOTTISH PUBLISHER,
JAMES ELPHINSTONE, ON THE DEATH OF
ELPHINSTONE'S MOTHER.
25 SEPTEMBER 1750.

Dear Sir,
You have, as I find by every kind of evidence, lost an excellent Mother;
and I hope you will not think me incapable of partaking of your grief.
I have a Mother, now eighty-two years of age, whom, therefore, I must
soon lose, unless it please God that she should rather mourn for me. I
read the letters in which you relate your Mother's death to Mrs. Strahan,
and think I do myself honour, when I tell you that I read them with
tears; but tears are neither to *you* nor to *me* of any further use, when
once the tribute of nature has been paid. The business of life summons
us away from useless grief, and calls us to the exercise of those virtues
of which we are lamenting our deprivation. The greatest benefit which
one friend can confer upon another, is to guard and excite, and elevate
his virtues. This your mother will still perform, if you diligently preserve the memory of her life, and of her death; a life so far as I can learn,
useful, wise, and innocent; and a death resigned, peaceful, and holy. I
cannot forbear to mention, that neither reason nor revelation denies you
to hope, that you may increase her happiness by obeying her precepts;
and that she may, in her present state, look with pleasure upon every act
of virtue to which her instruction or example have contributed. Whether
this be more than a pleasing dream, or a just opinion of separate spirits,
is, indeed, of no great importance to us, when we consider ourselves as
acting under the eye of God: yet, surely, there is something pleasing in
the belief, that our separation from those whom we love is merely cor-
poreal; and it may be a great incitement to virtuous friendship, if it can
be made probable, that that union that has received divine approbation
shall continue to eternity.

There is one expedient by which you may, in some degree, continue her presence. If you write down minutely what you remember of her from your earliest years, you will read it with great pleasure, and receive from it many hints of soothing recollection when time shall remove her yet further from you, and your grief shall be matured to veneration. To this, however, painful for the present, I cannot but advise you as to a source of comfort and satisfaction in the time to come; for all comfort and all satisfaction is sincerely wished you by, dear Sir

Your most obliged, most obedient and most humble servant

Sam Johnson

See note appended to LETTER TWENTY.

LETTER TWENTY

DR JOHNSON TO JAMES BOSWELL ON THE DEATH
OF BOSWELL'S FATHER.
FROM LONDON, SEPTEMBER 1782.

Dear Sir,
I have struggled through this year with so much infirmity of body, and
such strong impressions of the fragility of life, that death, whenever it
appears, fills me with melancholy, and I cannot hear without emotion of
the removal of anyone, whom I have known, into another state.

Your father's death had every circumstance that could enable you to
bear it; it was a mature age, and it was expected; and as his general life
had been pious, his thoughts had doubtless for many years been turned
upon eternity. That you did not find him sensible must doubtless grieve
you; his disposition towards you was undoubtedly that of a kind, though
not a fond father. Kindness, at least actual, is in our power, but fondness
is not; and if by negligence or imprudence you had extinguished his
fondness, he could not at will rekindle it. Nothing then remained between you but mutual forgiveness of each other's faults, and mutual
desire of each other's happiness.

I received your letter only this morning.
I am dear Sir,
Yours etc.
Sam Johnson

*John Wain in his excellent book on Samuel Johnson (1709–84) describes the
letter to Elphinstone as 'masterly . . . He brings together all the thoughts that
can possibly strengthen a man in this situation and goes on to give some sound
practical advice.'*

*Johnson, there is no doubt about this, was and still is loved. There have been
other geniuses, there have been other wits, but those qualities only attract ad-*

miration and approval. The Johnson venerators tend to smile affectionately at the thought of him. It is the warmth and kindness and occasional absurdity of the man that attracts them. His faults are our faults too; we understand him and he would have understood us. In short, he was the most human of human beings.

Notable among his works were his satirical poems, London *and* The Vanity of Human Wishes, *his edition of Shakespeare, the periodical* The Rambler *and his* Dictionary of the English Language. *But his fame largely owes its permanence to the genius of his self-appointed biographer, James Boswell, who gives us a meticulously detailed portrait of the great man who had become his friend and mentor.*

From Boswell's Life of Johnson, *London, 1949.*

LETTER
TWENTY-ONE

HORACE WALPOLE TO HIS FRIEND GEORGE
MONTAGU ON THE DEATH OF MONTAGU'S
SISTER.
FROM LONDON, 7 OCTOBER 1755.

My dear Sir,
Nobody living feels more for you than I do: nobody knows better
either the goodness or tenderness of your heart, or the real value of the
person you have lost. I cannot flatter myself that anything I could say
would comfort you under an affliction so well founded; but I should
have set out, and endeavoured to share your concern, if Mrs. Trevor had
not told me that you were going into Cheshire. I will only say, that if
you think change of place can contribute at all to divert your melancholy, you know where you would be most welcome; and whenever
you will come to Strawberry Hill, you will, at least, if you do not find a
comforter, find a most sincere friend that pities your distress, and would
do anything upon earth to alleviate your misfortune. If you can listen
yet to any advice, let me recommend to you to give up all thoughts of
Greatwerth, you will never be able to support life there any more. Let
me look for some little box for you in my neighbourhood. You can
live nowhere where you will be more beloved; and you will there always have it in your power to enjoy company, or solitude, as you like.
I have long wished to get you so far back into the world, and now it
has become absolutely necessary for your health and peace. I will say no
more, lest too long a letter should either be troublesome or make you
think it necessary to answer; but do not, till you find it more agreable
to vent your grief this way than in any other.
    I am, my good Sir, with hearty concern and affection,
        Yours most sincerely,

At Eton and King's College Walpole had the poet Gray as a friend, and al-
though a Member of Parliament, was not a very active Member and preferred
to write light verses and letters and collect works of art. His closest friends at
Cambridge were George and Charles Montagu. Much of his life he lived in
Arlington Street, but in 1747 bought Strawberry Hill a 'country Box' in
Twickenham, called by him his 'Gothic Castle' and 'curiosity shop'; originally
only five acres it finally extended to fourteen, and Walpole enjoyed the planting
and cultivation. In 1753 he had a refectory, and library, and cloister added. He
lived from 1717–97.

From Letters to G. Montagu by Horace Walpole, *London, 1819.*

LETTER TWENTY-TWO

FROM MRS M. HARTLEY TO BARON ROKEBY ON
THE DEATH OF MRS MONTAGU.
SEPTEMBER 1800.

To you, my dear friend, the death of Mrs. Montagu must be a grief, as
well as a great loss; for you were in a situation to enjoy her friendship
and society.

When I read the article in the papers, it gave me an instant feeling of
regret that I should never see her more; but when I began to consider
the great improbability, that (if she had lived) we should ever have met
again; I perceived that I ought only to think of the event as it had a
reference to her. With regard to this life, she had passed through the
best of her days; those which were approaching must have been gloomy
and oppressive; and when the feat of life is completed, happy are those
who retire before the dregs are drawn off. Age and infirmities, like any
other must be endured with patience, if it please God to prolong life;
but if he thinks fit to take a virtuous person to an earlier rest, it is a
happy escape from pain and sorrow. Yet these are considerations of
small importance, in comparison of the state into which the spirit shall
pass after it is severed from its mortal clay. If that be happy, how infinitely would be the gain, although taken from the highest pinnacle of
youth and prosperity! If miserable, how poor a reprieve would be the
longest period that ever was given to human life! The escape, therefore,
from future misery, and the admission to future happiness, is the only
object which can engage a wise man's wishes and endeavours. The
period of life and the manner of death, we must leave to providence.
  'Nor love thy life, nor hate; but what thou liv'st
  Live well; how long or short submit to Heav'n'.

As my intercourse with Mrs. Montagu was never very intimate, I knew more of her intellectual abilities, than of her virtues. It was impossible to be in her company for an hour without perceiving the superiority of her genius; the brilliancy of her wit, the elegance of her taste (I mean in literature *not* in dress); the extent of her information; and the engaging, polite, and easy style of her address. Never have I been more entertained and delighted than with her conversation, when she has been so kind as to visit me; and never was she more sprightly and brilliant, or more kind and engaging than in the last visit she made me. I shall remember the entertainment of that pleasant hour as long as I live.

Mary Hartley (1737–1803) was a writer and philanthropist. She was the daughter of Dr Hartley of Illingworth in Yorkshire, and was intelligent, well-read, and a scholar in Latin, Greek, French and Italian. She died after suffering from prolonged 'pain, sickness and permanent decripitude' says Rebecca Warner in the volume noted below.

Elizabeth Montagu (1720–1800) was the sister of Matthew Robinson-Morris, second Baron Rokeby, and she was an authoress well known in society. She was thought by some to be a blue-stocking but Dr Johnson 'thoroughly enjoyed a conversation with her.' As well as entertaining the King and Queen in 1791, and regarding herself as the hostess of intellectual society, she also found time to entertain the local young chimney sweeps and feed them on roast beef and plum pudding.

From Mary Hartley: Original Letters, *edited by Rebecca Warner, London, 1817.*

LETTER
TWENTY-THREE

WILLIAM COWPER TO THE REVD JOHN NEWTON
ON THE DEATH OF NEWTON'S DAUGHTER.
16 OCTOBER 1785.

My dear Friend,
To have sent a child to Heaven is a great honour and a great blessing,
and your feelings on such an occasion may well be such as render you
rather an object of congratulation than of condolence. And were it
otherwise, yet, having yourself free access to all the sources of genuine
consolation, I feel that it would be little better than impertinence in me
to suggest any. An escape from a life of suffering to a life of happiness
and glory, is such a deliverance as leaves no room for the sorrow of
survivors, unless they sorrow for themselves. We cannot, indeed, lose
what we love without regretting it; but a Christian is in possession of
such alleviations of that regret, as the world knows nothing of. Their
beloveds, when they die, go they know not whither; and if they suppose
them, as they generally do, in a state of happiness, they have yet but an
indifferent prospect of joining them in that state hereafter. But it is not
so with you. You both know whither your beloved has gone, and you
know that you shall follow her; and you know also that in the meantime
she is incomparably happier than yourself.
　　Sincerely yours,
　　W.C.

*William Cowper (1731–1800) was educated at Westminster School and was
called to the Bar in 1754. He was, however, more interested in literary pursuits
than the law. After fits of depression, attempted suicide and a period of madness, when for over a year he lived in a private madhouse, he retired from*

London and lived in Huntingdon and finally Olney in Buckinghamshire. The curate there was John Newton, and Cowper worked with him in the parish and wrote the famous Olney Hymns. ('O for a closer walk with God', 'Hark, my soul, it is the Lord', 'Jesus, where'er thy people meet', 'God moves in a mysterious way'.)

When he had another breakdown John Newton was very kind to him, and Cowper lived in his house for more than a year. After his recovery Newton encouraged him to publish his early poems. In 1779 Newton became Rector of Woolnoth. Later Cowper was to publish The Task, John Gilpin, and various translations.

From The Life and Works of William Cowper, by Robert Southey, London, 1836.

LETTER
TWENTY-FOUR

GEORGE WASHINGTON TO HIS WIFE ON THE
DEATH OF A GRANDCHILD.
24 JUNE 1776.

My dearest Life and Love,
I congratulate you most cordially on the fair prospect of your amiable
daughter-in-law; nor can I wonder, that this second loss of a little one
should affect you, I fear the fatigues of the journey, and the perpetual
agitations of a camp, were too much for her. They are, however, both
young and healthy; so that there can be little doubt of their soon re-
pairing the loss.

My heart tells me that there never was a moment in my life, since I
first knew you, in which it did not cleave and cling to you with the
warmest affection: and it must cease to beat, ere it can cease to wish for
your happiness, above anything on earth.

George Washington (1732–99), first President of the United States of America.
*After the Americans had won their independence, there was a move to
establish their own monarchy and offer Washington the crown. It was not only
his career that made him the obvious choice. Early in life, through the death of
his brother, he had a vast estate to farm, and this had brought him into conflict
with the Indians and the French, in campaigns which proved him to be a military leader of the first rank and led to his appointment as Commander-in-Chief
of the united forces in the war against Great Britain. But it was his character,
his fortitude and nobility of mind that enabled him to contend not only with
enemy forces but with the discordant factions from which support had to come.
It was these qualities that secured for him the Presidency by the unaminous
votes of the newly appointed Electoral College.*
*It is significant that he tolerated but disapproved of slavery, and when he
died instructions were left to free all his own slaves.*
From George Washington Epistles, *New York, 1976.*

LETTER
TWENTY-FIVE

THOMAS JEFFERSON TO JOHN ADAMS ON THE
DEATH OF HIS WIFE, ABIGAIL ADAMS.
FROM MONTICELLO, 13 NOVEMBER 1818.

The public papers, my dear friend, announce the fatal event of which
your letter of October the 20th had given me ominous foreboding.
Tried myself in the school of affliction, by the loss of every form of con-
nection which can rive the human heart, I know well, and feel what you
have lost, what you have suffered, are suffering, and have yet to endure.
The same trials have taught me that for ills so immeasurable, time and
silence are the only medicine. I will not, therefore, by useless condolences, open afresh the sluices of your grief, nor, although mingling
sincerely my tears with yours, will I say a word more where words are
vain, but that it is of some comfort to us both, that the term is not very
distant, at which we are to deposit in the same cerement, our sorrows
and suffering bodies, and to ascend in essence to an ecstatic meeting with
the friends we have loved and lost, and whom we shall still love and
never lose again. God bless you and support you under your heavy
affliction.

Thomas Jefferson, 1743–1826, was the third President of the United States.
John Adams was the second President.
Jefferson wrote many letters to John Adams, though political differences
caused a break in the correspondence at one stage. Jefferson was the head of the
Republican party, and John Adams was a Federalist.
Jefferson was married himself in 1772 to Martha Wayles Skelton, who
died in 1782 soon after the birth of their second daughter Maria, who died
c.1802. He never forgot his wife.
From The Life and Selected Writings of Thomas Jefferson, *edited by*
Adrienne Koch and William Peden, New York, 1944.

LETTER
TWENTY-SIX

GOETHE TO FRAU SCHULTHEIS TEXTOR ON
THE DEATH OF HER HUSBAND - GOETHE'S
GRANDFATHER.
FROM STRASBOURG, FEBRUARY 1771.

Dearest Grandma,
The death of our dear father, already dreaded from day to day for so
long a time, has yet come upon me unprepared. I have felt this loss with
all my heart; and what to us is the world around us, when we lose what
we love?

To console myself, and not you, I write to you, you who are now
the head of our family to beg you for your love, and assure you of my
tenderest devotion. You have lived longer in the world than I, and must
find in your own heart more comfort than I know of. You have endured more misfortune than I; you must feel far more vividly than I
can say it, that the most sorrowful occurrence often, through the hand
of Providence, takes the most favourable turn for our happiness; that
the succession of fortune and misfortune in life is inter-twined like sleep
and waking, neither without the other, and one for the sake of the
other; that all happiness in the world is only lent. You have seen children
and grand-children die before you, ceasing their work in the morning
of their life; and now your tears accompany a husband to the everlasting
sabbath-rest – a man who has honestly earned his wage. He has it now;
and yet the good God, whilst he took thought for him has also taken
thought for you – for us. He has taken from us not the merry friendly,
happy old man who carried on the affairs of the age with the vivacity of
a youth, who stood out amongst his fellow-citizens and was the joy of
his family. He has now taken from us a man whose life we have seen for

some years hanging by a silken thread. His energetic spirit must have felt with painful heaviness the oppressive weight of a sickly body; must have wished himself free, as a prisoner yearns to escape from his cell.

Now he is free, and our tears bid him God-speed; and our sorrow gathers us around you, dear Mama, to console ourselves with you, hearts simply full of love. You have lost much, but much remains to you. Look at us, love us, and be happy. May you enjoy for a long time yet the temporal reward which you have so richly earned of our invalid father, who has gone hence to report it at the place of requital and who has left us behind as tokens of his love, tokens of the past time of sorrowful yet pleasing recollection.

And so may your love for us remain as it was; and where much love is, there is much happiness.

I am, with a truly warm heart your loving grandchild.

J. W. Goethe.

See note for LETTER TWENTY-SEVEN *below.*

LETTER
TWENTY-SEVEN
FROM GOETHE TO ZELTER ON THE DEATH OF
ZELTER'S YOUNGEST SON, THEN AGED SIXTEEN.
WEIMAR, 26 MARCH 1816.

This is indeed another hard task you have been allotted; sadly it is
always the old story that to live long means no more than to outlive
many, and in the end one never discovers what else it should have meant.
A few days ago, the first edition of my 'Werther' happened to come
into my hands again, and this song, long since dead and gone from my
thoughts, began to come to life again, and it seems incomprehensible
how a man can have put up for another forty years with living in a
world which had seemed so absurd to him even in his early youth. But
a part of that riddle is solved by the fact that everyone has within him
something of his very own which he hopes to develop by letting it
work and go on working in him. This mysterious being gets the better
of us and leads us on day by day, till we are old without knowing how
and why. On closer inspection, I find that it is the talent within me and
that alone which has been helping me through all the adverse circumstances in which I get entangled by false direction or by coincidence or
by confusion.
    May God keep you.
      Goethe

*In 1771 Goethe was 21. In that year he had obtained his doctor's degree at
Leipzig University, after spending most of 1769 recovering from a serious
illness. Son of a lawyer, he could not himself feel any interest in the law; he
longed to be creative; he was often moody and depressed, with strong religious
feeling.*

A BOOK OF CONDOLENCES

By 1816 he had written most of his great works. In that year, too, his wife died. As the years passed, more and more of his friends died, but he was cared for to the end by his beloved daughter-in-law and died peacefully in his arm-chair.

Goethe's grandfather, Johan Wolfgang Textor, was Chief Magistrate and an Imperial Councillor of Frankfurt; he died aged 78.

From Letters of J. W. Goethe, *London, 1846* – LETTER TWENTY-SIX. Goethe's Schönste Briefe, *Leipzig, 1930, translated by Hildburg Braun* – LETTER TWENTY-SEVEN.

LETTER TWENTY-EIGHT

FROM SAMUEL TAYLOR COLERIDGE TO CHARLES
LAMB ON THE DEATH OF LAMB'S MOTHER.
28 SEPTEMBER 1796.

Your letter, my friend, struck me with a mighty horror. It rushed upon me and stupified my feelings. You bid me write you a religious letter; I am not a man who would attempt to insult the greatness of your anguish by any other consolation. Heaven knows, that in the easiest fortunes there is much dissatisfaction and weariness of spirit; much that calls for the exercise of patience and resignation; but in storms, like these, that shake the dwelling and make the heart tremble, there is no middle way between despair and the yielding up of the whole spirit unto the guidance of faith. And surely it is a matter of joy, that your faith in Jesus has been preserved; the Comforter that should relieve you is not far from you. But as you are a Christian, in the name of that Saviour, who was filled with bitterness and made drunken with wormwood, I conjure you to have recourse in frequent prayer to his God and your God, the God of mercies, and father of all comfort. Your poor father is, I hope, almost senseless of the calamity; the unconscious instrument of Divine Providence knows it not, and your mother is in heaven. It is sweet to be roused from a frightful dream by the song of birds, and the gladsome rays of the morning. Ah, how infinitely more sweet to be awakened from the blackness and amazement of a sudden horror, by the glories of God manifest, and the hallelujahs of angels.

As to what regards yourself, I approved altogether of your abandoning what you justly call vanities. I look upon you as a man, called by sorrow and anguish and a strange desolation of hopes into quietness, and a soul set apart and made peculiar to God! we cannot arrive at any portion of heavenly bliss without in some measure imitating Christ. And they arrive at the largest inheritance who imitate the most difficult parts of his character, and bowed down and crushed under foot cry in fullness of faith 'Father, thy will be done'.

I wish above measure to have you for a little while here – no visitants shall blow on the nakedness of your feelings – you shall be quiet, and your spirit may be healed. I see no possible objection, unless your father's helplessness prevent you, and unless you are necessary to him. If this be not the case, I charge you write me that you will come.

I charge you, my dearest friend, not to dare to encourage gloom or despair – you are a temporary sharer in human miseries, that you may be an eternal partaker of the Divine nature. I charge you, if by any means it be possible, come to me.

I remain, your affectionate,
    S. T. Coleridge

Charles Lamb's reply follows – LETTER TWENTY-NINE. *For notes see* LETTER THIRTY-ONE.

LETTER
TWENTY-NINE

CHARLES LAMB TO SAMUEL TAYLOR COLERIDGE
IN REPLY (SEE LETTER TWENTY-EIGHT
PRECEDING).
3 OCTOBER 1796.

My dearest friend, Your letter was an inestimable treasure to me. It will comfort you I know to know that our prospects are somewhat brighter. My poor dearest Sister, the unhappy and unconscious instrument of the Almighty Judgements to our House, is restored to her senses; to a dreadful sense and recollection of what has past, awful to her mind, and impressive (as it must be to the end of life) but tempered with religious resignation and the reasonings of a sound judgement which in this early stage knows how to distinguish between a deed committed in a transient fit of frenzy and the terrible guilt of a Mother's murder. I have seen her. I found her this morning calm and serene, far, very far, from an in-decent forgetful serenity; She has a most tender and affectionate concern for what has happened . . . . God be praised, Coleridge, wonderful as it is to tell, I have never once been otherwise than collected and calm; even on the dreadful day and in the midst of the terrible scene I pre-served a tranquility which by-standers may have construed into indif-ference, a tranquility not of despair; is it folly in me or sin to say that it was a religious principle that *most* supported me. I allow much to other favourable circumstances. I felt that I had something else to do than to regret; On that first evening my aunt was lying insensible to all ap-pearance like one dying – my father, with his poor forehead plastered over from a wound he had received from a daughter dearly loved by him who loved him no less dearly, – my Mother a dead and murdered corpse in the next room – yet I was wonderfully supported.

These mentioned good fortunes and change of prospects had almost brought my mind over to the extremes the very opposite to despair; I was in danger of making myself too happy; your letter brought me back to a view of things which I had entertained from the beginning; I hope (for Mary I can answer) but I hope that I through life shall never have less recollection nor a fainter impression of what has happened than I have now; 'tis not a light thing, nor meant by the Almighty to be received lightly. I must be serious, circumspect, and deeply religious through life; by such means may *both* of us escape madness in future, if it so please the Almighty.

Send me word how it fares with Sara. I repeat it, your letter was and will be an inestimable treasure to me; you have a view of what my situation demands of me like my own view; and I trust a just one.

See LETTER THIRTY-ONE.

LETTER THIRTY

CHARLES LAMB TO WILLIAM WORDSWORTH ON
THE DEATH BY DROWNING OF WORDSWORTH'S
BROTHER.
 18 FEBRUARY 1805.

My dear Wordsworth,
The subject of your letter has never been out of our thoughts since the
day we first heard of it, and many have been our impulses towards you,
to write to you, or to write to enquire about you; but it never seemed
the time. We felt all your situation, and how much you would want
Coleridge at such a time, and we wanted somehow to make up to you
in his absence, for we loved and honoured your Brother, and his death
always occurs to my mind with something like a feeling of reproach,
as if we ought to have been nearer acquainted and as if there had been
some incivility shown him by us, or something short of that respect
which we now feel; but this is always a feeling when people die, and I
should not foolishly offer a piece of refinement instead of sympathy, if I
knew any other way of making you feel how little like indifferent his
loss has been to us.
 Charles Lamb

See LETTER THIRTY-ONE.

LETTER
THIRTY-ONE

SAMUEL TAYLOR COLERIDGE TO JOHN PIERSE
KENNARD ON THE DEATH OF HIS FRIEND
ADAM STEINMETZ.
THE GROVE, HIGHGATE, 13 AUGUST 1832.

My dear Sir,
Your letter has announced to me a loss too great, too awful, for common
grief, or any of its ordinary forms and outlets. For more than one hour
after, I remained in a state which I can only describe as a state of deepest
mental silence. Neither prayer nor thanksgiving, but a prostration of
absolute faith, as if the Omnipresent were present to me by a more
special intuition, passing all sense and all understanding. Whether Death
be but the Cloudy Bridge to the Life beyond, and Adam Steinmetz has
been wafted over it without suspension, or with an immediate resump-
tion of self-conscious existence, or whether his Life be hidden in God,
in the eternal only-begotten, the Pleroma of all Beings and the Habita-
tion both of the Retained and the Retrieved, therein in a blessed and
most divine slumber to grow and evolve into the perfected Spirit, – for
sleep is the appointed season of all growth here below, and God's ordi-
nances in the earthly may shadow out his ways in the Heavenly, – in
either case our friend is *in God* and *with God*. Were it possible for me
even to *think* otherwise, the very grass in the fields would turn black
before my eyes, and nature appear as a skeleton fantastically mossed
over beneath the weeping vault of a charnel house!
  Deeply am I persuaded that for every man born on earth there is an
appointed task, some remedial process in the soul known only to the
Omnicient, and, this through divine grace fulfilled, the sole question is
whether it be needful or expedient for the Church that he should still

remain; for the individual himself 'to depart and to be with Christ', must needs be GREAT again.

Charles Lamb (1775–1834), Samuel Taylor Coleridge (1772–1834), and William Wordworth (1770–1850) were closely associated all of their lives.

Lamb and Coleridge were at school together at Christ's Hospital; Coleridge and Wordsworth had met in 1796, and, as outcome of their discussion together on the principles of poetry, the Lyrical Ballads *were planned and published in 1800. Coleridge's contribution was* The Ancient Mariner. *In 1805 Coleridge was abroad.*

John Pierse Kennard was the friend of Adam Steinmetz, a friend and ardent disciple of Coleridge in his later years.

John Wordsworth was Captain of the East Indiaman Earl of Abergavenny *which was wrecked off Portland Bill on 5 February 1805. 200 persons being lost. He was only 33.*

From The Second Treasury of the World's Great Letters, *London, n.d.* – LETTER TWENTY-EIGHT. The Letters of Charles Lamb, *edited by E. V. Lucas, London, 1935* – LETTERS TWENTY-NINE *and* THIRTY. The Letters of Samuel Taylor Coleridge, *edited by Kathleen Raine, London, 1950* – LETTER THIRTY-ONE.

LETTER THIRTY-TWO

DANIEL WEBSTER TO HIS SECOND WIFE,
CAROLINE WEBSTER, ON THE DEATH OF
HER SISTER.
MONDAY MORNING, 15 FEBRUARY 1830.

My dear Caroline,
I suppose we receive just about the same time the melancholy tidings of
the death of your dear sister. Altho' it was so fearfully expected, it yet
is a great shock to learn the reality & certainty of what was so much
dreaded. I have the news in a letter from your father, which I enclose
to you, although he has probably written as fully to you as to me.
   Her friends have the consolation of knowing that all was done for her,
which kindness & affection could do, as well as that her excellent
principles & sober & thoughtful character & feelings have prepared
her for the change. Her daughter will doubtless feel the loss most deeply,
she has always been so much with her mother, & has left her home
recently.
   Yrs ever constantly
   Daniel Webster

A note follows LETTER THIRTY-THREE.

LETTER
THIRTY-THREE

DANIEL WEBSTER TO EDWARD P. LITTLE ON
THE DEATH OF MRS LITTLE.
MARSHFIELD, 25 SEPTEMBER 1852.

My dear Sir,
I deeply sympathise with you & your children, in the affliction, which
you & they suffer, in the loss of a wife & mother, whose life was so
invaluable to you & to them and who was so much an object of respect
& love, to all who knew her. I earnestly commend you & yours to
patience & trust in God.

I shall most gladly speak most warmly of yr. estate – to any one whom
may think of buying. I regard it as one of the landmarks in the town,
containing good lands & buildings, well cultivated & fruitful, situated
in the bank of the river, a short distance from the sea.
　　　Your friend
　　　D. Webster

*Daniel Webster (1782–1852), a farmer's son, was admitted to the bar in 1805,
later becoming a congressman and senator. At heart a simple country gentleman,
he was full of sympathy and concern for friends and relations in trouble.*

*Webster married Caroline Le Roy in December 1829. He had had four
children by his first wife, who died in January 1828.*

*Mr Little had written to Webster of the death of his wife and had asked him
for help in finding a purchaser for his farm; he and Webster were neighbours
in Marshfield.*

From The Letters of Daniel Webster, *edited by C. H. Van Tyne, New
York, 1902.*

LETTER THIRTY-FOUR

LEIGH HUNT TO JOSEPH SEVERN – SENT IN THE
BELIEF THAT KEATS WAS STILL ALIVE AND THAT
IT COULD BE COMMUNICATED TO HIM.
HAMPSTEAD, 8 MARCH 1821.

Dear Severn,
You have concluded, of course, that I have sent no letters to Rome
because I am aware of the effect they would have on Keats's mind; and
this is the principal cause, – for besides what I have been told of his
emotions about letters in Italy, I remember his telling me on one occasion, that in his sick moments, he never wished to receive another
letter, or even to see another face however friendly. But still I should
have written to you had I not been almost at death's door myself. You
will imagine how ill I have been when you hear that I have but just
begun writing again for the *Examiner* and *Indicator*, after an interval of
several months, during which my flesh wasted from me in sickness and
melancholy. Judge how often I thought of Keats, and with what feelings. Mr. Brown tells me he is comparatively calm now, or rather quite
so. If he can bear to hear of us, pray tell him – but he knows it already
and can put it in better language than any man. I hear he does not like
to be told that he may get better; nor is it to be wondered at, considering
his firm persuasion that he shall not recover. He can only regard it as a
puerile thing, and an insinuation that he cannot bear to think he shall
die.

But if this persuasion should happen no longer to be so strong upon
him, or if he can now put up with such attempts to console him, remind
him of what I have said a thousand times, and that I still (upon my
honour, Severn), think always, that I have seen too many instances of

recovery from apparently desperate cases of consumption, not to indulge in hope to the very last. If he cannot bear this, tell him – tell that great poet and noble-hearted man – that we shall all bear his memory in the most precious parts of our hearts, and that the world shall bow their heads to it, as our loves do. Or, if this again will trouble his spirit, tell him we shall never cease to remember and love him and that the most sceptical of us has faith enough in the high things that nature puts into our heads, to think that all who are of one accord in mind and heart, are journeying to one and the same place, and shall meet somehow or other again, face to face, mutually conscious, mutually delighted. Tell him he is only before us on the road, as he was in everything else, or whether you tell him the latter or no, tell him the former and add that we shall never forget he was so, and that we are coming after him. The tears are again in my eyes and I must not afford to shed them – the next letter I write shall be more to yourself, and a little more refreshing to your spirits, which we are very sensible must have been greatly taxed. But whether our friend dies or not, it will not be among the least lofty of our recollections by-and-by, that you helped to smooth the sick-bed of so fine a being.

  God bless you, dear Severn,
    Your sincere friend,
    Leigh Hunt.

Leigh Hunt (1784–1859) met John Keats (1795–1821) in 1816 and from then on he, Keats, went frequently to his house where he met Shelley. His first poems were published in The Examiner, *a newspaper run by Leigh Hunt and his brother John.*

 Joseph Severn (1793–1879) was another devoted friend of Keats' and was then a struggling art student with musical talent and a love of literature.

 In 1820 Keats was already ill with consumption and was advised to spend the winter in Italy. Severn wished to study in Rome, so they set out together and, as his illness progressed, Severn nursed Keats faithfully to the end.

 From The Correspondence of Leigh Hunt, *edited by His Eldest Son, London, 1862.*

LETTER
THIRTY-FIVE

LORD BYRON TO JOHN M. B. PIGOT ON THE
DEATH OF BYRON'S MOTHER.
FROM NEWPORT PAGNELL, 2 AUGUST 1811.

My Dear Doctor – My poor mother died yesterday and I am on my
way from town to attend her to the family vault. I heard one day of her
illness, the next of her death. – Thank God her last moments were most
tranquil. I am told she was in little pain and not aware of her situation. –
I now feel the truth of Mr. Gray's observation, 'That we can only have
one mother.' – Peace be with her! I have to thank you for your expression of regard, and as in six weeks I shall be in Lancashire on business, I may extend to Liverpool and Chester, – at least I shall endeavour.

I shall remain at Newstead the greater part of this month, where I
shall be happy to hear from you, after my two years' absence in the
East.

I am dear Pigot, yours very truly,
Byron.

See LETTER THIRTY-SEVEN

LETTER THIRTY-SIX

LORD BYRON TO SCROPE BERDMORE DAVIES ON
THE DEATH OF CHARLES SKINNER MATTHEWS.
NEWSTEAD ABBEY, 7 AUGUST 1811.

My dearest Davies – Some curse hangs over me and mine. My mother
lies a corpse in this house; one of my best friends is drowned in a ditch.
What can I say, or think, or do? I received a letter from him the day
before yesterday. My dear Scrope, if you can spare a moment, do come
down to me, I want a friend. Matthews' last letter was written on
Friday, – on Saturday he was not. In ability, who was like Matthews?
How did we all shrink before him? You do me but justice in saying, I
would have risked my paltry existence to have preserved his. This very
evening did I mean to write, inviting him, as I invite you, my very dear
friend, to visit me. God forgive . . . for his apathy. What will our poor
Hobhouse feel! His letters breathe but of Matthews. Come to me
Scrope, I am almost desolate – left almost alone in the world – I had but
you and H[obhouse] and M[atthews] and let me enjoy the survivors
whilst I can. Poor M in his letter of Friday, speaks of his intended con-
test for Cambridge, and a speedy journey to London. Write or come,
but come if you can, or one or both.

Yours ever.

See LETTER THIRTY-SEVEN.

LETTER THIRTY-SEVEN

LORD BYRON TO JOHN HOBHOUSE ON THE
DEATH OF THEIR FRIEND CHARLES SKINNER
MATTHEWS, HIS FRIEND J. WINGFIELD AND
BYRON'S MOTHER.
NEWSTEAD ABBEY, 10 AUGUST 1811.

My dear Hobhouse – From Davies I had already received the death of
Matthews, and from M a letter dated the day before his death. – In
that letter he mentions you, and as it was perhaps the last he ever wrote,
you will derive a poor consolation from hearing that he spoke of you
with that affectionate familiarity, so much more pleasing from those we
love, than the highest encomiums of the World. – My dwelling, you
already know, is the House of Mourning, and I am really so much be-
wildered with the different shocks I have sustained, that I can hardly
reduce myself to reason by the most frivolous occupations. – My poor
friend, J. Wingfield, my Mother, and your best friend, and (surely not
the worst of mine) C[harles] S[kinner] M[atthews] have disappeared in
one little month since my return, and without my seeing either, though
I have heard from All. – There is to me something so incomprehensible
in death, that I can neither speak or think on the subject. – Indeed when
I looked on the Mass of Corruption, which was the being from whence
I sprang, I doubted within myself whether I was, or She was not, – I
have lost her who gave me being, and some of those who made that
Being a blessing. – I have neither hopes nor fears beyond the Grave, yet
if there is within us a 'spark of that Celestial Fire' M[atthews] has already
'mingled with the Gods'. – In the room where I now write (flanked by
the Skulls you have seen so often) did you and M and myself pass some
joyous unprofitable evenings, and here we will drink to his Memory,

which though it cannot reach the dead, will soothe the Survivors, and to them only death can be an Evil. – I can neither receive or administer Consolation. Time will do it for us, in the Interim let me see or hear from you, if possible both. – I am very lonely, and should think myself miserable, were it not for a kind of hysterical merriment, which I can neither account for, or conquer, but, strange as it is, I do laugh and heartily, wondering at myself while I sustain it. – I have tried reading and boxing, and swimming, and writing, and rising early and sitting late, and water, and wine, with a number of ineffectual remedies, and here I am, wretched, but not 'melancholy or gentlemanlike' – My dear, 'Cam of the Cornish' (M's last expression) may Man or God give you the happiness, which I wish rather than expect you may attain; believe me none living are more sincerely yours than Byron –

George Gordon Byron (1788–1824) was born in Aberdeen, but most of his life, when not abroad, he lived in England. Newstead Abbey was his ancestral home. His mother spent several summers at Southwell in Nottinghamshire, in those days an inland watering place. Here Byron was introduced to John Pigot, a medical student from Edinburgh.

Scrope Davies, Charles Matthews and John Hobhouse were Byron's contemporaries at Cambridge, and were close friends. Charles Matthews was drowned when bathing alone among the reeds of the Cam.

John Wingfield was a friend of Harrow days and died at Coimbra in 1811.

From Byron's Letters and Journals, *edited by Leslie A. Marchand, London, 1973.*

LETTER THIRTY-EIGHT

FROM THE LETTERS OF DIRECTION OF IVANOV MACARIUS TO A WIDOW.

I thank you for having unveiled to me the sadness of your grief-stricken heart; a great radiance comes over me when I share with others their sorrow. Complete, perfect, detailed compassion is the only answer I can give to your tender love of me that has led you, at such a time, to seek me out in my distant silent, humble hermitage.

Christ says, as it were: I accepted the cross for the salvation of mankind; and whomsoever I specially long to draw unto myself, on him do I first pierce with arrows dipped in the wormwood of grief. This I do so that he may die to the extreme fascination, to the sweetness, of transitory joys and powers. The scourge of sorrows is the banner of my love. Thus did I wound the heart of my servant David; but when the stream of tribulations had separated him from the world, then did a dread Meditation, an unwanted, blessed trend of thought well up in his mind and take full possession of his whole being.

In the ground of the Christian's heart, sorrow for the dead soon melts, illumined by the light of the true wisdom. Then, in the place of the vanished grief, there shoots up a new knowledge made of hope and faith. This knowledge does not only wash the soul of all sadness; it makes it glad.

Fanaticism shackles the mind; faith gives it the wings of freedom. This freedom is apparent in a quiet firmness, unruffled by any circumstances, fortunate or unfortunate. The sword that cuts us free of shackles is the purified mind; the mind that has learnt to discern the true, the secret, the mysterious cause and purpose of every occurrence. Purification of the mind is gained through frequently pondering on one's utter insignificance; but this pondering should always be veiled in a throbbing living prayer: for God's protection and his help.

Macarius (1788–1860) was a Staret – that is, a spiritual director of priests, monks and lay people. Starets – the word is derived from Starik, *the Russian for 'Old Man' – are accorded more than the veneration with which an 'elder' is conventionally regarded. One is called to be a staret only after a long life devoted to the cultivation of simplicity and humility. 'The way – for himself and his disciples – lies through obedience and prayer, and it exacts a constantly deepening love of God and all creatures.'*

From The Russian Letters of Direction of Ivanov Macarius, *selected and edited by Julia de Beausobre, Moscow, 1888.*

LETTER THIRTY-NINE

FROM LAMARTINE TO COUNT RAIGECOURT ON
THE DEATH OF RAIGECOURT'S MOTHER.
MACON, 21 MARCH 1832.

My dear Raoul,

The blow which you have sustained has struck me forcibly too. You know that, when you were still only a child, I was already like a son for your wonderful mother and that she acted towards me and guided me as she would have done for you. I have never found in any woman such kindly, sustained and motherly feelings towards me. I had become accustomed to considering her as the earliest member of that type of honorary family which kindred feeling and gratitude create for us when we are solitary wanderers in the world, far from the wings of our real family. So her loss leaves in my thoughts and heart, as also in the happy pattern of my Parisian days, a gap which can never be filled. I am reaching the time of life when these gaps are multiplied daily to detach us little by little from a world where only regrets are bound to be durable.

Although you are so young, you have already experienced many sore trials: your strong spirit will be further fortified by them. But this moral strength which suffering gives us by tempering us in its flames cannot alas equal that straightforward and tender affection which we bring into this world and which ought to be enjoyed longer with objects worthy of love. All the same you have still much left to love; a wonderful father, children whom I hear are delightful, and sisters, one of whom will take the place of a mother, for you if need be, and for your children. Her heart, devoted entirely to others, has kept back for itself only pity for everyone. How overwhelmed she must be!

I was greatly touched by the kindness of Madame de Lascases who informed me so speedily of the sad event. I see she understood that no one would be more affected by it nor have the sad right to share in it sooner and more completely. Thank her again from me.

I shall visit you probably two months from now, before leaving for Constantinople. It will be a sad and painful occasion for me.

Keep a bit of your mother's tenderness for me, all of you. It is my portion of her inheritance and I shall never renounce it.

Lamartine.

Alphone Lamartine (1790–1869) was born into a Royalist family and played a great part in the turbulent politics of his day, and in the end became a Republican. When Napoleon III came to power he retired from politics and devoted his life to writing.

His first volume of poems Méditations *was published in 1820 and brought him immediate fame: and on the publication of* Harmonies poétiques et religieuses *he was unanimously elected to the Academy. His tour to the East produced* Souvenirs d'Orient.

Lamartine was a Romantic poet. In his poems he escaped from reality, and his poems have been described by Geoffrey Brereton as 'murmured reveries'. His most well-known poem, Le Lac, *is based on his own feeling and experience of love.*

From Lamartine Correspondence Générale, *edited by M. Lavaillant, Paris, 1943.*

LETTER FORTY

FROM MRS CARLYLE TO HER COUSIN HELEN
WELSH, ON THE DEATH OF HER FATHER.
CHELSEA, WEDNESDAY, 12 OCTOBER 1853.

Dearest Helen,

I know not what I am going to say, I am quite stupefied. I had somehow
never taken alarm at my Uncle's illness. I had fixed my apprehensions
on the journey home, and was kept from present anxiety by that far off
eve. My beloved Uncle, all that remained to me of my mother. A braver
more upright, more generous hearted man never lived. When I took
leave of him in Liverpool and he said 'God bless you dear' (he had never
called me dear before) I felt it was the last time we should be together,
felt that distinctly for a few hours; and then the impression wore off,
and I thought I would go back soon, would go by the cheapest train
(God help me), since it gave him pleasure to see me. That we have him
no longer is all the grief! It was well he should die thus, gently and
beautifully, with all his loving kindness fresh as a young man's; his
enjoyment of life not wearied out; all our love for him as warm as
ever; and well he should die in his own dear Scotland, amid quiet kindly
things. We cannot, ought not to wish it had been otherwise, to wish he
had lived on till his loss should have been less felt.

But what a change for you all, and for me too, little as I saw of him
to know that kind, good Uncle was in the world for me, to care about
me, however long absent, as nobody, but one of his own blood can, was
sweetness in my lonely life, which can be ill-spared.

Poor dear little Maggie, I know how she will grieve about these two
days and think of them, more than of all the years, of patient, loving
nursing which should be now her best comfort. Kiss her for me. – God
support you all. Write to me when you can what you are going to do.
Alas, that I should be so far away from your councils. I need to know

precisely about your future in an economical sense; through all the dull grief that is weighing on me, comes a sharp anxiety lest you should be less independent than heretofore. To be relieved of that will be the best comfort you can give me at present. I never knew what money you had to live on, nor thought about it; now it is the first question I ask. I am dreary and stupid, and can write no more just now.

Your affectionate

J.C.

[Postscript] When I saw your handwriting again last night, my only thought was, 'how good of her to write another letter soon'. It was long before I could UNDERSTAND it.

Jane Welsh Carlyle (1801–66) was the wife of the historian Thomas Carlyle. The daughter of a doctor, Jane was born in Scotland and known in her village as 'The Flower of Haddington'. In 1826, she married Carlyle, writer, critic and creative historian. They quarelled incessantly and few doubt that he treated her badly; he had warned her of his 'dark humours', she in turn had a 'sharp tongue.' The marriage was by no means a complete failure. The first years of their life together were particularly unhappy ones for her and on reading her diaries and letters after her death he suffered greatly from remorse. Her letters reveal an acute sensibility and critical zest. The first collection was published in 1883 and there have been recent further editions.

From Jane Welsh Carlyle: A Selection of Her Letters, *edited by Trudy Bliss, London, 1950.*

LETTER
FORTY-ONE

FROM RALPH WALDO EMERSON TO THOMAS
CARLYLE ON THE DEATH OF HIS WIFE, JANE
CARLYLE.
CONCORD, 16 MAY 1866.

My dear Carlyle,
I have just been shown a private letter from Moncure Conway to one
of his friends here, giving some tidings of your sad return to an empty
home. We had the first news last week. And so it is. The stroke long
threatened has fallen at last, in the mildest form to its victim, and relieved to you by long and repeated reprieves. I must think her fortunate
also in this gentle departure, as she had been in her serene and honoured
career. We would not for ourselves count covetously the descending
steps, after we have passed the top of the mount, or grudge to spare
some of the days of decay. And you will have the peace of knowing
her safe and no longer a victim. I have found myself recalling an old
verse which one utters to the parting soul, –

> For thou has passed all change of human life,
> And not again to thee shall beauty die.

It is thirty years, I think, since I last saw her, and her conversation and
faultless manners gave assurance of a good and happy future. As I have
not witnessed any decline, I can hardly believe in any, and still recall
vividly the youthful wife and her blithe account of her letters and
homages from Goethe, and the details she gave of her intended visit to
Weimar, and its disappointment. Her goodness to me and to my friends
was ever perfect and all Americans have agreed in her praise. Elizabeth
Hoar remembers her with entire sympathy and regard.

I could heartily wish to see you for an hour in these lonely days. Your friends, I know, will approach you as tenderly as friends can; and I can believe that labor – all whose precious secrets you know – will prove a consoler – though it cannot quite avail – for she was the rest that rewarded labor. It is good that you are strong, and built for endurance. Nor will you shun to consult the aweful oracles which in these hours of tenderness are sometimes vouchsafed. If to any, to you.

I rejoice that she stayed to enjoy the knowledge of your good day at Edinburgh, which is a leaf we would not spare from your book of life. It was a right manly speech to be so made, and is a voucher of unbroken strength – and the surroundings, as I learn, were all the happiest – with no hint of change. I pray you bear in mind your own counsels. Long years you must still achieve, and, I hope, neither grief nor weariness will let you 'join the dim choir of the bards that have been,' until you have written the book I wish and wait for – the sincerest confessions of your best hours. My wife prays to be remembered to you with sympathy and affection.

> Ever yours faithfully,
> R. W. Emerson.

Ralph Waldo Emerson (1803–82), minister and writer, known as the Sage of Concord because of his lectures, essays and poems.

Emerson first met the Carlyles in 1832, and stayed with them in England. The Carlyles never got to Weimar due to the miscarriage of his book on German Literature.

Jane Carlyle died on 19 April 1866. Two days before she died, Carlyle, in Scotland, sent her a copy of his Inaugural Address which he had delivered at Edinburgh University on 2 April.

Moncure Conway was a friend of Emerson who acted as a sort of agent for the publishers, Harper & Brothers, in the publication of Emerson's letters.

The source of the quotation is unknown.

From The Letters of R. W. Emerson to Thomas Carlyle, edited by Joseph Slater, Columbia, 1964.

LETTER FORTY-TWO

LONGFELLOW TO MARY APPLETON MACKINTOSH
IN ANSWER TO A LETTER FROM HER ON THE
DEATH OF HIS WIFE ELIZABETH WHO WAS MARY
APPLETON MACKINTOSH'S SISTER.
NAHANT, 18 AUGUST 1861.

Dearest Mary,

I will try to write you a line today, if only to thank you for your affectionate letter, which touched and consoled me much.

How I am alive after what my eyes have seen, I know not. I am at least patient, if not resigned; and thank God hourly – as I have from the beginning – for the beautiful life we led together, and that I loved her more and more to the end.

Truly do you say there was no one like her. And now that she is gone, I can only utter a cry 'from the depth of divine Despair'. If I could be with *you* for a while, I should be greatly comforted, only to you can I speak out all that is in my heart about her.

It is a sad thing for Robert to have been here through all this. But his fortitude and his quiet sympathy have given us all strength and support. How much you must have needed him! He goes back to you with our blessing, leaving regrets behind. We all love him very much.

I am afraid I am very selfish in my sorrow; but not an hour passes without my thinking of you, and of how you will bear the double woe, of a father's and a sister's death at once. Dear affectionate old man!
The last day of his life, all day long, he sat holding a lily in his hand, a flower from Fanny's funeral. I trust that the admirable fortitude and patience which thus far have supported you, will not fail. Nor must you think, that having preached resignation to others I am myself a castaway.

Infinite tender memories of our darling fill me and surround me. Nothing but sweetness comes from her. That noble, loyal, spiritual nature always uplifted and illumined mine and always will, to the end.

Meanwhile think of me here by this haunted sea-shore. So strong is the sense of her presence upon me, that I should hardly be surprised to meet her in our favourite walk, or, if I looked up now, to see her in the room.

My heart aches and bleeds sorely for the poor children. To lose *such* a mother, and all the divine influences of her character and care. They do not know how great their loss is, but I do. God will provide. His will be done! Full of affection, ever most truly,

    H W L

Henry Wadsworth Longfellow (1807–82) was educated at Bowdoin and at Harvard, became professor of modern languages at Bowdoin and in 1836 at Harvard. His prose romance Hyperion *and first volume of poems* Voices in the Night *were published in 1839, and followed by* Ballads and other Poems *containing* Excelsior *and* The Wreck of the Hesperus, Evangeline, The Golden Legend, Hiawatha *and many others; in 1872* Christus *a trilogy appeared, which Longfellow considered his greatest achievement.*

In July 1843 Longfellow married Elizabeth Appleton, the original of the heroine of Hyperion. *The happiness of their marriage is witnessed by this letter to his sister-in-law.*

In July 1861, Longfellow was in his study while his wife, in the adjoining library, was sealing small packets of her two younger daughters' hair with burning wax. Her dress caught on fire. Her husband tried unsuccessfully to wrap her in a rug. She died the next day. He himself received burns.

Longfellow visited England in 1842 and stayed with his friend Charles Dickens. His popularity in England is proved by the erection of a monument to him in Westminster Abbey.

From Longfellow Trust Collection.

LETTER FORTY-THREE

JOHN GREENLEAF WHITTIER TO WILLIAM LLOYD
GARRISON ON THE DEATH OF HIS WIFE.
AMESBURY, 10 FEBRUARY 1876.

My dear Garrison,
I know that words avail little in some of the great trials and bereavements of life, but I cannot forbear expressing my sympathy with thee at this time. The termination, with her saintly life, of the intimate communion and association which, for so many years, have been enjoyed by thyself and thy dear wife, must leave thee lonely and sad at times, and I would fain reach out a hand to thee.

I know what it is to sit alone, like a stranger, at my own hearth; but as time passes on, the memory of my dear friends grows more sweet and precious, and the hope of soon meeting them makes the great inevitable change more tolerable to contemplate.

God has been good to thee in giving thee such a loving and faithful and excellent companion for so many years; and now thy children and children's children gather close about thee. And, with thy spiritual views, it may be that a realizing sense is afforded thee, that the dear one is still living, and still near thee!

A line from our mutual friend Harriet Pitman tells me that thee are, or have been, quite ill thyself. I trust, ere this reaches thee, thy health will be better, if not fully restored.

With much love thy old friend
John G. Whittier.

John Greenleaf Whittier (1807–92) was a Quaker and a poet and with William Lloyd Garrison he worked for the abolition of slavery.

All of Whittier's letters show he had great faith in a God of mercy and love, and he hoped for personal immortality. He says in a letter to Edna Dean Proctor, 'There is no great use in arguing the question of immortality. One must feel its truth. You cannot climb into Heaven on a syllogism.'

In a letter to Elizabeth Lloyd Howell he says, 'Oh this mystery of Death! How dark and fearful it would be but for our faith in Divine Goodness.'

To Joseph Liddon Pennock he quotes 'a beautiful thought of Charles Follen on the loss of friends: "It is the enduring nature of true sorrow which forms the connexion between Time and Eternity; it is the burden of its Divine appointment to induce us to seek in Heaven that which we have lost on earth".'

From The Letters of John Greenleaf Whittier, *edited by John B. Pickard, Harvard, 1975.*

LETTER
FORTY-FOUR

ABRAHAM LINCOLN TO THE FATHER AND
MOTHER OF COLONEL ELMER F. ELLSWORTH
WHO HAD DIED IN THE CIVIL WAR.
WASHINGTON DC, 25 MAY 1861.

My dear Sir and Madam,
In the untimely loss of your noble son, our affliction here is scarcely less
than your own. So much of promised usefulness to one's country, and
of bright hopes for one's self and friends, have rarely been so suddenly
dashed as in his fall. In size, in years, and in youthful appearance a boy
only, his power to command men was surpassingly great. This power,
combined with a fine intellect, an indomitable energy, and a taste altogether military, constituted in him, as seemed to me, the best natural
talent in that department I ever knew.

And yet he was singularly modest and deferential in social intercourse.
My acquaintance with him began less than two years ago; yet through
the latter half of the intervening period it was as intimate as the dis-
parity of our ages and my engrossing engagements would permit. To
me he appeared to have no indulgences or pastimes; and I never heard
him utter a profane or an intemperate word. What was conclusive of
his good heart, he never forgot his parents. The honors he laboured for
so laudably, and for which in the sad end he so gallantly gave his life,
he meant for them no less than for himself.

In the hope that it may be no intrusion upon the sacredness of your
sorrow, I have ventured to address you this tribute to the memory of
my young friend and your brave and early fallen child.

May God give you that consolation which is beyond all earthly
power.

Sincerely your friend in a common affliction,
A. Lincoln.

*Abraham Lincoln (1809–65) was the sixteenth President of the United States.
He was born in Hardin County, Kentucky, the son of a western pioneer. In
1816 the family moved to the forests of Indiana. Until he was nineteen Abraham
was a farm worker. From 1840, now in Illinois, he became clerk in a store,
storekeeper, postmaster, and deputy county surveyor, studied law and grammar
and entered politics, and soon showed his ability as a debater. He rose to the
Presidency in 1860. During the Civil War Lincoln procured the emancipation
of the slaves. In 1864 he became President for a second term. He was assas-
sinated at Ford's Theatre in 1865 by the actor John Wilkes Booth, a member
of a wide-ranging conspiracy.*

*He married Mary Todd at Springfield and had four sons, only one of whom
survived to manhood. He ever strove to be a man of peace, and all through the
Civil War, wanted one battle to end all the strife. He lost his son Willie
in 1862.*

From Abraham Lincoln: The Complete Works, Speeches, Letters and
State Papers, *Volume One, edited by John G. Nicolay and John Hay, New
York, 1894.*

LETTER
FORTY-FIVE

FROM GLADSTONE TO ALFRED LYTTLETON ON
THE DEATH OF HIS WIFE.
29 APRIL 1886.

My dear Alfred,

It is a daring and perhaps selfish thing to speak to you at a moment when your mind and heart are a sanctuary, in which God is speaking to you in tones even more than usually penetrating and solemn.

Certainly it pertains to few to be chosen to receive such lessons as are being taught you. If the wonderful trials of Apostles, Saints and Martyrs have all meant a love in like proportion wonderful then, at this early period of your life, your lot has something in common with theirs, and you will bear upon you life-long marks of a great and peculiar dispensation which may and should lift you very high. Certainly you two who are still one were the persons whom in all the vast circuit of London life those near you would have pointed to as exhibiting more than any others the promise and the profit of both worlds. The call upon you for thanksgiving seemed greater than on anyone – you will not deem it lessened now. How eminently true it is of her than in living a short time she fulfilled a long time. If life is measured by intensity, hers was a very long life – and yet with that rich development of mental gifts, purity and singleness made her one of the little children of whom and of whose like is the Kingdom of Heaven. Bold would it be indeed to say that she died prematurely. All through your life however it be prolonged, what a precious possession to you she will be. But in giving her to your bodily eye and taking her away the Almighty has specially set his seal upon you. To peace and to God's gracious mercy let us heartily, yes cheerfully, commend her. Will you let Sir Charles and Lady Tennant and all her people know how we feel with and for them.

    Ever your affec.
      W. E. Gladstone

W. E. Gladstone (1809–98) was four times Prime Minister, alternating with Conservative Leaders from 1868 to 1892. He was a classical scholar of the highest rank and frequent contributor to the learned reviews. Above all he was a practical Christian and had an abiding interest in rescuing prostitutes from the streets.

    Alfred Lyttelton held office under Gladstone, and apart from his distinguished political career was renowned for his charm and prowess in every kind of ball game.

LETTER FORTY-SIX

EXTRACT FROM A LETTER FROM CHARLES
DICKENS TO JOHN FORSTER ON THE DEATH OF
FORSTER'S ONLY BROTHER.
GENOA, 8 FEBRUARY 1845.

I feel the distance between us now, indeed. I would to Heaven, my
dearest friend, that I could remind you in a manner more lively and
affectionate than this dull sheet of paper can put on, that you have a
Brother left. One bound to you by ties as strong as ever Nature forged.
By ties never to be broken, weakened, changed in any way – but to be
knotted tighter up, if that be possible, until the same end comes to them
as has come to these. That end but the bright beginning of a happier
union, I believe; and have never more strongly and religiously believed
(and oh! Forster, with what a sore heart I have thanked God for it) than
when that shadow has fallen on my own hearth, and made it cold and
dark as suddenly as in the home of that poor girl you tell me of. When
you write to me again , the pain of this will have passed. No consolation
can be so certain and so lasting to you as that softened and manly sorrow
which springs up from the memory of the Dead. I read your heart as
easily as if I held it in my hand, this moment. And I know – I *know*, my
dear friend – that before the ground is green above him, you will be
content that what was capable of death in him, should lie there. I am
glad to think it was so easy, and full of peace. What can we hope for
more, when our own time comes! – The day when he visited us in our
old house is as fresh to me as if it had been yesterday. I remember him as
well as I remember you . . . I have many things to say, but cannot say
them now.

Your attached and loving friend for life, and far, I hope, beyond it.

When Charles Dickens (1812–70) and John Forster first met Dickens was a *rising young author with* The Pickwick Papers *appearing in monthly instalments and earning a popularity which increased with every instalment.*
  Forster, younger than Dickens by just two months, was already a literary critic of considerable influence in that make-or-break world.
  The two became lifelong friends and the relationship enabled Forster to be a great and frequent help to the impulsive and passionate genius, though the warmth which illuminates this letter was not always so conspicuous.
  In 1842 Dickens went to America, where he advocated international copyright and the abolition of slavery.
  In that year he published his American Notes.
  In 1867–8 he gave public readings in England and America.
  From Forster's Life of Dickens, *by John Forster, London, 1873.*

LETTER FORTY-SEVEN

CHARLOTTE BRONTE TO ELLEN NUSSEY ON THE DEATH OF ANNE CARTER WHO HAD BEEN A PUPIL OF CHARLOTTE.
12 JANUARY 1840.

Your letter, which I received this morning, was one of painful interest. Anne Carter it seems, is *dead;* when I saw her last she was a young, beautiful and happy girl; and now 'life's fitful fever' is over with her and she 'sleeps well'. I shall never see her again. It is a sorrowful thought for she was a warm-hearted, affectionate being, and I cared for her. Where ever I seek her now in this world she cannot be found, no more than a flower or a leaf which withered twenty years ago. A bereavement of this kind gives one a glimpse of the feeling those must have who have seen all drop round them, friend after friend, and are left to end their pilgrimage alone. But tears are fruitless, and I try not to repine.

Charlotte Bronte (1816–55), the novelist, was the daughter of an Irish clergyman who had accepted a living at Haworth village on the Yorkshire Moors in 1821. At the age of eight Charlotte was sent with her sisters to Cowan Bridge School, where two of her sisters became ill and died.

Her first successful novel Jane Eyre *was based on her experiences in the School.*

Her brother Branwell died in September 1848, her sister Emily, author of Wuthering Heights, *died in December 1848, and her remaining sister Anne died in 1849. She was then left alone with her austere melancholy father. She continued to write and produced* Shirley *in 1849 and in 1852* Villette *which was her own favourite.*

In 1854 she married her father's Curate and enjoyed, in spite of continuous ill-health, the rest of her short life. According to Mrs Gaskell, Charlotte's friend and biographer, she suffered from the Celtic temperament, alternate high spirits followed by long periods of depression.

In another letter to a close friend, Ellen Nussey, dated 1852, Charlotte wrote – 'Submission, Courage, exertion when practicable – these seem to be the weapons with which we must fight life's long battle.' When confronted herself with tragedy upon tragedy these indeed where the weapons she used.

Anne Carter was a young pupil of Charlotte's who had been at school with Anne Bronte.

From The Life of Charlotte Bronte, *by Mrs Gaskell, London, 1924.*

LETTER FORTY-EIGHT

JAMES RUSSELL LOWELL TO CHARLES F. BRIGGS
ON THE DEATH OF HIS LITTLE DAUGHTER
BLANCHE.
ELMWOOD, 30 AUGUST 1844.

My dear Friend – I did not get your letter of the 19th until yesterday,
or you may be sure that I should have written sooner to assure you (if
words are needful) of my fullest and tenderest sympathy. Maria sends
hers also, and there are tears in the eyes of both of us.

I agree entirely with what you have said of Death in your last letter;
but at the same time I know well that the first touch of his hand is cold,
and that he comes to us, as the rest of God's angels do, in disguise. But
we are enabled to see his face fully at last, and it is that of a seraph. So
it is with all. Disease, poverty, death, sorrow, all come to us with un-
benign countenances; but from one after another the mask falls off, and
we behold faces which retain the glory and the calm of having looked
in the face of God. To me, at least, your bereavement has come with
softest step, and the most hallowed features, for it has opened a new
channel for my love to flow towards you in. More, it has made my
heart tenderer and more open to all, and I can even almost believe that I
love Maria better, as I forecast how she and I may be called upon to bear
the same trial together. The older I grow, the less am I affected by the
outward observances and forms of religion, and the more confidingness
and affection do I feel towards God. 'He leadeth me in green pastures.'
Trust in Providence is no longer a meaningless phrase to me. The
thought of it has oftener brought happy tears into my eyes than any
other thought except that of my beloved Maria. It is therefore no idle
form when I tell you to lean on God. I know that it is needless to say this

to you, but I know also that it is always sweet and consoling to have our impulses seconded by the sympathy of our friends.

I could not restrain my tears when I read what you say of the living things all around the cast mantle of your child. It *is* strange, almost awful, that, when this great miracle has been performed for us, Nature gives no sign. Not a bee stints his hum, the sun shines, the leaves glisten, the cock-crow comes from the distance, the flies buzz into the room, and yet perhaps a minute before the most immediate presence of God of which we can conceive was filling the whole chamber, and opening its arms to 'suffer the little one to come unto Him.'

God bless you a thousand times and comfort you, for He only can. I know not what I can say to your wife.

    Most lovingly yours,
      J. R. L. and M. W.
I shall write again soon.

James Russell Lowell (1819–91) was a poet, essayist, Harvard professor, editor of The Atlantic Monthly *and, with C. E. Norton, the* American Review.

    Lowell met Charles Briggs in New York in 1842. He, like Lowell, was a writer, actively contributing to the magazines of the day.

    From The Letters of James Russell Lowell, *edited by C. E. Norton, New York, 1894.*

LETTER FORTY-NINE

EXTRACT FROM A LETTER TO MRS CHARLES
BRAY FROM GEORGE ELIOT ON THE DEATH OF
THE BRAYS' ADOPTED DAUGHTER.
18 MARCH 1865.

I don't know whether you strongly share, as I do, the old belief that
made men say the gods loved those who died young. It seems to me
truer than ever now life has become more complex and more and more
difficult problems have to be worked out. Life, though a good to men
on the whole, is a doubtful good to many, and to some not at all. To
my thought, it is a source of constant mental distortion to make the
denial of this a part of religion, to go on pretending things are better
than they are . . . So to me, early death takes the aspect of salvation –
though I feel too that those who live and suffer may sometimes have the
greater blessedness of *being* a salvation.

See the note for LETTER FIFTY.

LETTER FIFTY

EXTRACT FROM A LETTER FROM MRS M. E.
LEWES (GEORGE ELIOT) TO MRS TROLLOPE
THANKING HER FOR HER CONDOLENCE LETTER.
LONDON, 19 DECEMBER 1879.

I have never told you how grateful I was to you for writing to me a year
ago. For a long while I could read no letter. But now I have read yours
more than once and it is carefully preserved. You had been with us in
our happiness so near the time when it left me – you and your husband
are peculiarly bound up with the latest memories.

*George Eliot (1819–80) was the pen name of Mary Ann (Marian) Evans, one
of the greatest of Victorian novelists.*

*The Brays were long standing friends of George Eliot's. It was to the
influence of Charles Bray, whom she first met in 1840, that she was freed from
her excessively narrow religious beliefs. He was a Coventry manufacturer with
intellectual interests and unorthodox views on religion. One of the most important events in her life took place ten years later when she met, and fell in
love with, the gifted and versatile writer, George Henry Lewes. As a person he
was amusing, generous and kind, possessing a social conscience and a good
sense of values all of which qualities were bound to appeal to George Eliot.
Knowing that he was already married and for various reasons unable to obtain
a divorce, she took her courage in both hands and in 1854 she went to live with
him as his common-law wife. It proved a very happy union which lasted
until his death in 1878. She then became desperately depressed but was fortunate in having innumerable good friends, in particular Charles Cross whom
she married only a few months before she died.*

*Sensitivity, unconventional wisdom and learning were perhaps George
Eliot's main characteristics. As a writer she was a creative genius and considered one of England's most distinguished novelists.*

Anthony Trollope's mother was a very remarkable woman. To support the family, at fifty, she took to writing. Her first book, about the American way of life, was a best seller. Anthony tells us in his Autobiography *that when she died, at the age of seventy-six, she had written 114 books.*

From The George Eliot Letters, *edited by G. S. Haight, Oxford, n.d.—* LETTERS FORTY-NINE *and* FIFTY.

LETTER FIFTY-ONE

EXTRACT FROM A LETTER BY QUEEN VICTORIA
TO GENERAL GORDON'S SISTER ON HIS DEATH.

How shall I write to you, or how shall I attempt to express what I feel!
To think of your dear Brother, who served his Country and his Queen
so truly, so heroically, with a self sacrifice so edifying to the World, not
having been rescued. That the promises of support were not fulfilled –
which I so frequently, and constantly pressed on those who asked him to
go – is to me a grief inexpressible! indeed, it has made me ill . . . Would
you express to your other sisters and your elder Brother my true sympathy, and what I do so keenly feel, the stain left upon England, for
your dear Brother's cruel, though heroic, fate!

*Queen Victoria (1819–1901) of Great Britain and Ireland, Empress of India.
She ascended the throne in 1837. Proud author of* Leaves from a Journal of
our life in the Highlands *and an extensive writer of letters in which she
characteristically used underlining as a rhetorical weapon.*

*In this letter to Gordon's sister she is expressing the popular reaction to the
news of his death. Since then, historians have given us a different view of the
man. Put quite simply, Gordon had the British Government's instructions to
evacuate Khartoum under threat from the vast fanatical forces of the Mahdi.
When surrounded, and with a relieving British Expeditionary force drawing
near, he said 'I am not the rescued Lamb and I will not be. I will stay here
and fall with the town and run all risks.'*
From Eminent Victorians, Lytton Strachey, London, 1928.

LETTER FIFTY-TWO

FROM MARY BAKER EDDY TO PRESIDENT
MCKINLEY'S WIDOW ON THE DEATH OF THE
PRESIDENT.
PLEASANT VIEW, NH, 14 SEPTEMBER 1901.

My dear Mrs. McKinley: – My soul reaches out to God for your support, consolation, and victory. Trust in Him whose love enfolds thee. 'Thou wilt keep him in perfect peace whose mind is stayed on Thee: because he trusteth in Thee.' 'Out of the depths have I cried unto Thee.' Divine Love is never so near as when all earthly joys seem most afar.

Thy tender husband, our nation's chief magistrate, has passed earth's shadow into Life's substance. Through a momentary mist he beheld the dawn. He awaits to welcome you where no arrow wounds the eagle soaring, where no partings are for love, where the high and holy call you again to meet.

'I know that Thou hearest me always,' are the words of him who suffered and subdued sorrow. Hold this attitude of mind, and it will remove the sackcloth from thy home.

With love,
Mary Baker Eddy

Mary Baker Eddy (1821–1910) was the founder of Christian Science and the author of Science and Health *(1875). She organized at Boston the Church of Christ Scientist (1879) to 'reinstate primitive Christianity and its lost element of healing.'*

From The First Church of Christ, Scientist, and Miscellany, *Mary Baker Eddy, Boston, 1913.*

LETTER
FIFTY-THREE

MISS ELLEN WILLMOTT TO HERBERT COWLEY ON
THE DEATH OF GERTRUDE JEKYLL.
ESSEX, 9 DECEMBER 1932.

Dear Mr. Cowley,
I have just had a telegram from Lady Jekyll with the sad tidings of Miss
Jekyll's death. I am sure it will grieve you deeply, and I am full of sorrow at the loss of one I admired so greatly and loved sincerely. She was
such a sensitive and great personality. I so thoroughly realised it, perhaps more than others.

In her were all the qualities I most admire; for apart from being a
great gardener and lover of plants, her sense of beauty and the picturesque in a garden combined with horticulture and cultivation at its
best is very rarely found. In fact, I have never known it except in my
sister, Mrs. Berkely Spetchley.

It was always a matter of surprise to me that the many activities and
her different material and artistic achievements were all of the best and
highest.

I was fifteen when I first knew her. Then the awe she inspired in-me
in the course of years became admiration and affection. You who knew
her so well had so many opportunities of knowing her great attainments.
I saw her last in August just before I was taken ill with bronchial pneumonia. It was a great effort to go to Munstead but I had a feeling I must
go. Her last letter was upon Sir Herbert's death. On the occasion of my
last visit she mentioned that the notes I made about her and which you
published had given her more pleasure than have anything else written
about her. I gave an evening about her at the Garden Club with slides of
views of her garden. Several of her family were present and they all
seemed pleased.

Although the present generation of so-called gardeners knew her only as a name, to all of us who knew her she was always a living force, and example and inspiration.

It was Sir Herbert's death which must have hastened her death, for her last letter to me was very pathetic. Perhaps I may see you at the RHS on Tuesday.

E. Willmott

Gertrude Jekyll (1843–1932) is generally regarded as the greatest English gardener and garden planner of her day. She often worked with the architect Sir Edwin Lutyens.

Miss Ellen Wilmott was a close friend.

Sir Herbert Cowley was Gertrude Jekyll's brother and a gardener in his own right. Herbert Cowley was his son.

From Miss Jekyll: Portrait of a Great Gardener, *Betty Massingham, London, 1966.*

LETTER
FIFTY-FOUR

SIR WILLIAM OSLER, IN THE GUISE OF HIS DEAD
SON WHO DIED ONE WEEK OLD, SENDS A REPORT
OF LIFE IN HEAVEN TO MRS OSLER.
FEBRUARY, 1893.

If we are good and get on nicely with our singing and if our earthly
parents continue to show an interest in us by remembering us in their
prayers, we are allowed to write every three or four tatmas (i.e. month).
I got here safely with very little inconvenience. I scarcely knew anything until I awoke in a lovely green spot, with fountains and trees and
soft couches and such nice young girls to tend us. You would have been
amused to see the hundreds which came the same day. But I must tell
you first how we are all arranged; it took me several days to find out
about it. Heaven is the exact counterpart of earth, so far as its dwellers
are concerned, thus all from the U.S. go to one place – all from Mary-
land to one district and even all from the cities and townships get cor-
responding places. This enables the guardian angels to keep the lists
more carefully and it facilitates communication between relatives. They
are most particular in this respect and have a beautifully simple arrange-
ment by which the new arrivals can find out at once whether they have
connections in Heaven. I never was more surprised in my time – we say
that here, not life and not eternity for that has not started for us – when
the day after my arrival Althea brought me two quill feathers on one of
which was written Julius Caesar and the other Emma Osler. I knew at
once about the former . . . but the latter I did not know at all, but she
said she had been father's little sister and she had been sent to make me
feel happy and comfortable.

Unlike the real angels we have no fore-knowledge and cannot tell what is to happen to our dear ones on earth. Next to the great feast days, when we sing choruses by divisions in the upper Heavens, our chief delight is in watching the soul bodies as they arrive in our divisions and in helping the angels to get them in order and properly trained. In the children's divisions not a friad (i.e. about an hour of earthly time) passes without the excitement of a father or mother, a brother or a sister united to one of us. We know about 1000 of each other so that it is great fun to see our comrades and friends making their relatives feel at home.

Sir William Osler (1849–1919), the Canadian physician, was very fond of children and had a marked affinity with them. He enjoyed writing letters to them. One child described the secret of his success at a tea-party: 'He assured us (contrary to all previous teachings!) that the only enjoyable way of having bread and jam was a pile of jam on the plate with a few crumbs of bread on it, the whole of which one ate with a spoon.'

    He married Grace Revere Gross in 1892. They were extremely happy and it was a great blow when their first child died when only one week old. Mrs Osler found this letter on the dressing table one morning, it was addressed 'Dear Mother,' postmarked 'Heaven' and written by Paul Osler. Sir William and Lady Osler later had a son who was killed in the First World War.

    From A Treasury of the World's Great Letters, *edited by M. Lincoln Schoster, London, 1950.*

LETTER FIFTY-FIVE

ROBERT LOUIS STEVENSON TO CHARLES BAXTER
ON THE DEATH OF BAXTER'S FATHER.
  VAILIMA, SEPTEMBER 1894.

My dear Charles,
Well, there is no more Edmund Baxter now; and I think I may say I
know how you feel. He was one of the best, the kindest and the most
genial men I ever knew. I shall always remember his brisk, cordial ways
and the essential goodness which he showed me whenever we met with
gratitude. And the always is such a little while now! He is another of the
landmarks gone; and when it comes to my own turn to lay my weapons
down, I shall do so with thankfulness and fatigue; and whatever may be
my destiny afterwards, I shall be glad to lie down with my fathers in
honour. It is human at least, if not divine. And these deaths make me
think of it with an even greater readiness. Strange that you should be
beginning a new life when I who am a little your junior am thinking of
the end of mine. But I have had hard lines; I have been so long waiting
for death; I have unwrapped my thoughts from about life for so long,
that I have not a filament left to hold by; I have done my fiddling so
long under Vesuvius, that I have almost forgotten to play, and can only
wait for the eruption, and think it long of coming. Literally no man has
more wholly outlived life than I. And still it's good fun.

Robert Louis Stevenson (1850–94), the novelist and poet, was a master story-
teller who loved youth and adventure and disliked all forms of bourgeois re-
spectability. Hence, no doubt, his habit of wearing long hair and velvet coats,
a taste which matched his flamboyant character.
  This letter to his friend Charles Baxter was written three months before he

died. The last brave sentence is typical of the man who fought so valiantly and for so long, against ill health.

Charles Baxter was a close friend of Stevenson's at Edinburgh University, sharing with him in equal measure a taste for injudicious levity. He was described by Richard La Gallienne as 'a preposterously vital and imaginative talker, ample of frame, with a voice like a column of cavalry'. In spite of their mutually induced frivolous diversifications both passed their Law examinations with Distinction. Baxter became a Writer to the Signet and was latterly a dedicated guardian of Stevenson's financial interests. He was on his way to Samoa on a visit but had only reached Suez when Stevenson died.

From Robert Louis Stevenson: Letters to his Family and Friends, *edited by Sydney Colvin, London, 1900.*

LETTER
FIFTY-SIX

FROM G. B. SHAW TO MRS PATRICK CAMPBELL
ON THE DEATH OF HER SON, ACTING LIEUTENANT-
COMMANDER ALAN U. CAMPBELL, KILLED IN
ACTION ON 30 DECEMBER 1917.
LONDON, 7 JANUARY 1918.

Never saw it or heard about it until your letter came. It is no use: I can't
be sympathetic; these things simply make me furious. I want o swear.
I *do* swear. Killed just because people are blasted fools. A cha lai 1 too,
to say nice things about it. It is not his business to say nice th ng; about
it, but to shout that the 'voice of thy son's blood crieth untc G ,d from
the ground.'

No, don't show me the letter. But I should very much like to have a
nice talk with that dear Chaplain, that sweet sky-pilot, that . . .

No use going on like this, Stella. Wait for a week, and then I shall be
very clever and broadminded again and have forgotten all about this.
I shall be quite as nice as the Chaplain.

Oh, damn, damn, damn, damn, damn, damn, damn, damn, DAMN.

And oh, dear, dear, dear, dear, dear, dearest!

G.B.S.

*George Bernard Shaw (1856–1950) is equally well-known as a critic, novelist,
playwright, and socialist.*

Mrs Patrick Campbell (1865–1940) first made her name on the stage in
The Second Mrs Tanqueray.

*In her relationship with Bernard Shaw Mrs Patrick Campbell is best known
for creating the part of Eliza Doolittle in* Pygmalion. *Bernard Shaw found
her adorable but frequently exasperating. Their letters were as good as a play,*

and in fact have been successfully made into what could better be described as a stage entertainment. This letter shows that behind the pretence of passion there was in Shaw genuine affection and outraged sensibility.

From My Life and Some Letters, *by Mrs Patrick Campbell, London, 1922.*

LETTER
FIFTY-SEVEN

FROM GREY OF FALLODON TO HIS OLD FRIEND
DR PEMBER ON THE DEATH OF HIS SON EDWARD,
KILLED AS AN AIRMAN IN THE WAR.
6 OCTOBER 1917.

To Dr Pember – I see the news in today's paper. I am full of deep sympathy for you and your wife and daughter and my heart goes out in
earnest hope that you may be able to endure, and that you may be able
to support and comfort each other. I know very well that there is no
escape from the suffering of grief. We cannot love much without suffering much, and the very pain of the suffering is an evidence of the
strength of our love, so that we cannot even wish grief to be less than it
is and must be. The best I can wish for you is that you may have the
courage and strength: you yourself know just where to seek and find it.
Some of it you will get I hope from the thought of all the pleasure you
have had from Edward's life, and of his fine example. We who are left
have to be worthy of those from whom we are separated.

*Edward Grey, Viscount Grey of Fallodon (1862–1933), enjoyed an exception-
ally happy marriage which after twenty years came to an abrupt end. His wife
was killed driving a pony trap, the pony shied and she was thrown out stunned
and never recovered consciousness.*

G. M. Trevelyan in his book Grey of Fallodon *said, 'he did what was
right and wise in this crisis of his soul; he shouldered his work and he opened
his heart to his friends . . .'. His letters to his friends concealed nothing of his
sufferings for, again in Trevelyan's words, 'he was too close to nature to be*

reserved where there was no occasion, though he had in supreme degree a natural dignity, impressive without offence'.

Edward Grey was also a naturalist and author, and Foreign Secretary from 1905 until 1916.

From Grey of Fallodon, by G. M. Trevelyan, London, 1937.

LETTER FIFTY-EIGHT

CAPTAIN SCOTT TO J. M. BARRIE.
NEAR SOUTH POLE, MARCH 1912.

We are pegging out in a very comfortless spot. Hoping this letter may be found and sent to you, I write a word of farewell . . . More practically, I want you to help my widow and my boy – your godson.

Goodbye, I am not at all afraid of the end, but sad to miss many a humble pleasure which I had planned for the future on our long marches. I may not have proved a great explorer, but we have done the greatest march ever made and come very near to great success. Goodbye, my dear friend.

We are in a desperate state, feet frozen, no fuel and a long way from food; but it would do your heart good to be in our tent, to hear our songs and the cheery conversation as to what we will do when we get to Hut Point.

Later. We are very near the end, but have not and will not lose our good cheer. We have had four days of storm in our tent, and nowhere food or fuel. We did intend to finish ourselves when things proved like this, but we have decided to die naturally in the track.

As a dying man, my dear friend, be good to my wife and child. Give the boy a chance in life if the State won't do it. He ought to have good stuff in him.

I never met a man in my life whom I admired and loved more than you, and I never could show you how much your friendship meant to me, for you had much to give and I nothing.

Robert Falcon Scott (1868–1912) became a naval cadet in 1881. He was in command of the 1901–4 expedition to the Antarctic in the Discovery. *In 1906*

he was promoted Captain and set out in 1910 to carry out in the Terra Nova
*his plans for a second expedition, which culminated in the sledge journey to the
Pole, reached with Wilson, Oates, Bowers and Evans on 17 January 1912.
They fought their way back against atrocious weather condition, and the final
disaster closed in on them eight weeks later.*

Wilson wrote in one of his letters home: 'Scott is a man worth working
for as a man. No one can say that it will only have been a Pole-hunt. We *must
get to the Pole; but we shall get more too'. Prolonged blizzard conditions were
faced, for instance, to study the habits of the Emperor Penguin. Wilson's com-
ment was merely: Birdnesting at —62°F is a somewhat novel experience.*

*Scott was accepted by his superlative team as their natural leader. They
served him wholeheartedly, with little short of affection. Nothing reveals the
man's courage, thoughtfulness and innate nobility better than these last letters
which could be got to paper only after Scott had thawed out his fingers at an
improvised tin and wick lamp.*

*James Matthew Barrie (1860–1937), the novelist and dramatist, is perhaps
best known today as the creator of* Peter Pan. *Barrie and Scott first met when
both were already distinguished in their totally different ways. On that occasion they walked away together from the party they had been attending and
found themselves in a state of mutual envy, Barrie hankering after the experience and achievements of the man of action and Scott maintaining they
were as nothing beside the world of the imagination in which an author has his
being.*

From Scott's Last Expedition: Captain Scott's Own Story, *London,
1923.*

LETTER
FIFTY-NINE

CAPTAIN SCOTT TO MRS WILSON WHOSE HUS-
BAND WAS DYING AT HIS SIDE.
NEAR SOUTH POLE, MARCH 1912.

If this letter reaches you, Bill and I will have gone out together. We are very near it now, and I should like you to know how splendid he was at the end – everlastingly cheerful and ready to sacrifice himself for others, never a word of blame to me for leading him into this mess. He is not suffering, luckily – at least, only minor discomforts.

His eyes have a comfortable blue look of hope, and his mind is peaceful with the satisfaction of his faith in regarding himself as part of a great scheme of the Almighty. I can do no more to comfort you than to tell you that he died as he lived, a brave, true man – the best of comrades and staunchest of friends.

My whole heart goes out to you in pity.

Edward Adrian Wilson (1872–1912) was a surgeon, zoologist, and artist to the Discovery *Expedition of 1901–4 and the* Terra Nova *Expedition of 1910.*

Before and between his Antarctic labours he had led a full life, rowing and playing football with distinction at Cambridge and subsequently serving on the staff of hospitals and working also on commissions as a naturalist. For membership of an Antarctic team he had every qualification except good health; he had had a severe attack of tuberculosis, and on recovery was recommended a sedentary life. But then he was Edward Wilson.

From Scott's Last Expedition: Captain Scott's Own Story, *London,* 1923.

LETTER SIXTY

CAPTAIN SCOTT TO MRS BOWERS WHOSE SON
HENRY WAS DYING AT HIS SIDE.
NEAR SOUTH POLE, MARCH 1912.

We are very near the end of our journey, and I am finishing it in
company with two gallant, noble gentlemen. One of these is your son.
He had come to be one of my closest and soundest friends, and I appreciate his wonderful, upright nature, his ability and energy. As the
troubles have thickened, his dauntless spirit ever shone brighter, and he
has remained cheerful, hopeful, and indomitable to the end.

The ways of Providence are inscrutable, but there must be some
reason why such a young, vigorous and promising life is taken.

To the end he has talked of you and his sisters. One sees what a happy
home he must have had, and perhaps it is well to look back on nothing
but happiness. He remains unselfish, self-reliant and splendidly hopeful
to the end, believing in God's mercy to you.

*Lieutenant Henry R. 'Birdie' Bowers RN was a member of the team that
underwent the terrible winter journey to Cape Crozier in 1911.*

*Captain Scott commented on him 'never was there such a sturdy, active, un-
defeatable little man.' 'A short red-headed thick-set little man with a very large
nose' was Wilson's description of him, 'a perfect marvel of efficiency. But in
addition he has the most unselfish character I have ever seen in a man anywhere
. . . He takes the edge off a lot of difficulty for everyone by accepting everything
that is said to him as a matter of course in the most solemn manner imaginable;
when he always becomes irresistibly humorous, and there isn't a thing that happens that he doesn't find a ridiculous side to. He is a perfect treasure.'*

From Scott's Last Expedition: Captain Scott's Own Story, *London,*
1923.

LETTER SIXTY-ONE

FATHER ANDREW SDC TO A MOTHER WHOSE
SON AGED RATHER LESS THAN TWENTY-EIGHT
HAD COMMITTED SUICIDE.
APRIL 1907.

I don't fear for poor X in the least. I have got very strong positive beliefs, but no negative ones, and I am perfectly certain that God is much more beautiful than Religion. I think trials like this enable people to rise above Religion to God, and people who cannot unite in their religion, unite in Him. For Religion is, after all, only such a revelation of Himself as man has been able to see or conceive, and He is infinitely more beautiful and holy than we can dream or think.

So let your poor heart find rest as I have found rest in God Himself. Your love for your dear one is his Love in you, and really only the dimmest little reflection of His love. Half our prayers are expressions of doubt, not expressions of faith. We are always suggesting to God how he may love His people, as though we could teach Him to love, who ourselves have only just begun to dream what love is . . . We must just let the love in us, which is His life in us, grow more and more. The fact that your heart is just breaking with love and pity is the great revelation that God's love is overflowing towards you and yours. And in that love we are all one. It is a comfort to me to think that all things, religion included, have to be made to square with God, and not He with them. You know I speak with adoring reverence. He has shown Himself to me to be more beautiful and loving than any saint has ever dreamt. Be content that your boy has gone to Him.

Father Andrew (1869–1946) was a founder member of the Franciscan order of the Society of the Divine Compassion. After his death in 1946 some of his letters of direction were published, together with a memoir by Kathleen E. Burne.

From The Life and Letters of Father Andrew SDC, *edited by Kathleen E. Burne, Oxford, nd.*

LETTER SIXTY-TWO

FROM FATHER HUGHSON TO A SISTER ON THE DEATH OF HER HUSBAND.

My dearest B –
I was much distressed when I came home to find the telegram about Jack . . . Dear Jack – God rest his dear soul – his gentle thoughtfulness, his kindly loving spirit which seemed never to put self first, but always was full of thoughts for others. If I, who saw him so seldom, was impressed with his character, how much more must it have been a factor in your life through all the years in which God gave him to you. I wish I could be with you to tell all that is in my heart. I have been praying for you, and for him and you may be sure there will be no cessation in my prayers.

We believe that he is in God's holy keeping and that it is only a matter of time when we shall all be reunited in God and find that joy which comes from the consciousness that never again will there be any separation, for that union is in and with God, which he promises to us who seek to be faithful to the light that is given. Only last night in the account of the raising of Lazarus I was reading of the tender, infinite sympathy of our Lord with those who grieve. The whole account, as St John gives it, is a marvellous revelation of the love of God for His people, a love which is to us a pledge that in the end all will be well if we continue to seek Him and His love and righteousness. He enters into our griefs and infirmities. He teaches us how to bear them and shows us that in the bearing of them, we gain from Him ever more power and love, that in all these exigencies of life 'underneath are the everlasting arms.' His words to Martha have been an inexpressible comfort to millions of souls through all the ages and we find our comfort in them now. 'I am the resurrection and the life; he that believeth in me though he were dead, yet shall he live, and whosoever liveth and believeth in me shall never die.'

The passing from this life is not death; to those who have sought to follow Him, it is an awakening to eternal life. We follow indeed, so haltingly; there is so much that is not what we would wish it to be but God is 'full of compassion and mercy, long-suffering, plenteous in goodness and truth.' That 86th psalm is so wonderfully filled with the assurance of His love, that we can rest on it in faith, letting nothing disturb us.

God keep you my dearest child. Give my love to the girls and all the family.

Your loving brother,

See the note for LETTER SIXTY-THREE *following.*

LETTER
SIXTY-THREE

EXTRACT FROM A LETTER BY FATHER HUGHSON
TO AN UNKNOWN PERSON.
SOMETIME IN 1944.

Yes I shall miss my dear old friend very much. This coming autumn
will mark the completion of fifty years of our friendship. It is not often
that one is given the privilege of such a long association. But as one
goes through life and sees so many pass on to the other side, there comes
the ever-deepening realisation that the gulf is neither wide nor deep
between the souls at rest and those still on their pilgrimage. One is just
a little further along the way than others, but they are all in the same
way and all 'in Christ', there can be no separation there. Death is not
the close of one life, and the beginning of another. It is only another
stage of the same life, the further flowering of the life which is being
lived under the guidance of the Blessed Spirit. One cannot fail to feel
strongly the incentive to live well that we may not disappoint those
blessed ones of their hope of seeing us again where they wait for us in
their place of repose. Pray for his soul, although I cannot think that
one with so loving a spirit which embraced every one in its range so
lovingly, will be far from the vision of God.

*Father Hughson who died in 1949 was for nearly forty years Chaplain of the
Sisters of St Mary and Master of Novices and Superior in the Order of the
Holy Cross Monastery, New York.*
    From The Spiritual Letters of Father Hughson of the Order of the
Holy Cross, *New York and London, 1952.*

LETTER
SIXTY-FOUR

FROM JOHN SLOAN TO ELIZABETH YEATS ON
THE DEATH OF HER FATHER.
NEW YORK CITY, 7 FEBRUARY 1922.

My dear Miss Yeats – That great man your father is no longer with us;
we expected him to go – not the mysterious journey into the great
beyond – we expected him to go to Ireland but we had an unformed
hope that he would never go. He has gone, gone easily with serenity
and for me the world can never be the same – the great warm glow
has gone. But I should have felt the same had he left for Ireland – He
would then have been with you and not with us – now he is with us all.

His was a swift illness – hardly an illness – confined to his room one
day, to his bed one day and then away to take first rank among the poets
of the past.

We did love him and he loved us – We have the usual regrets – feel
that we did not see him enough – appreciate him enough, I think these
are the common regrets, moments of realization of how selfish is each
part played in the farce of life – some day we may play the drama, I
believe that will be nobler.

Let your sister and brothers know how deeply I sympathise with you
all.

The Church from which he was buried was full of his lovers, about
250 people there (with only 24 hours notice) and they each felt as I did,
that they had lost their father – I assure you that my own father's death
was not so great a loss to me. I was never as near to him as to John Butler
Yeats, we did not understand each other – and had the Puritan stand-
offishness – no love expressed, all repression.

A few score men such as your father in the world at any one time would cure its sickness – but our civilization produces other flowers – unsavoury blooms rank and poisonous – John Butler Yeats was one of the rare exceptions.

With etc –

John Sloan.

John Sloan was an artist and socialist and was a valued friend of J. B. Yeats who described him as 'a progressive man and therein the best kind of American.'

J. B. Yeats was a distinguished portrait painter and a member of the illustrious Anglo-Irish family celebrated for their artistic and literary achievements.

He spent many years in America and a remark of his, 'The Americans are the most human, that is the most affectionate, sympathetic and helpful people that ever lived,' was prompted by his gratitude to John Sloan and his sister.

From J. B. Yeats: Selected Letters, *edited by Joseph Hone, London, 1944.*

LETTER SIXTY-FIVE

HERMANN HESSE TO THOMAS MANN ON THE
DEATH OF THOMAS MANN'S SON, KLAUS, WHO
HAD COMMITTED SUICIDE IN CANNES.
26 MAY 1949.

Dear Herr Thomas Mann,
Like all your friends, we have received the sad news with consternation
and profound sympathy. We old people are used to having our friends
and travelling companions taken from us, but there is something terri-
fying about losing someone close to us belonging to the generation
which, we thought, would take our places when we go and in a measure
shield us from the eternal silence. That is hard to take.

I don't know much about how you stood to Klaus. I myself followed
his beginnings with attentive sympathy. Later on I was sometimes
troubled for your sake by the shortcomings of his literary efforts, but
today I find consolation in the thought that these efforts finally culminated in a fine valuable work, which surpassed them, his book on André
Gide. This book, which won the hearts of his friends and yours will
long survive its author.

In these days we are thinking more than ever of you and your wife.
We press your hands in heartfelt sympathy.
　　Yours ever,
　　Hermann Hesse.

See the note for LETTER SIXTY-SEVEN.

LETTER SIXTY-SIX

THOMAS MANN'S ANSWER TO HERMANN HESSE'S
LETTER (LETTER SIXTY-FIVE).
6 JULY 1949.

Dear Hermann Hesse,
My previous letter had hardly been mailed when, very belatedly, the
kind words from you and your wife about our Klaus's death arrived.
Many thanks to you both, from my family as well as myself.

The thought of this life cut short fills me with grief. My relations with
him were difficult and I often had a sense of guilt, for from the very
start my existence cast a shadow on his. As a young man in Munich he
was quite the rambunctious prince and much of what he did was offen-
sive. Later, in exile, he became much more serious and moral; he worked
hard, but too quickly and with too much facility, which accounts for
certain flaws and a certain sloppiness in his books. When the death urge
began to develop that contrasted so puzzlingly with his apparent sun-
niness, affability, ease, and charm, I don't know. Despite all the love and
help he was given, he persisted in destroying himself; in the end he
became incapable of any thought of loyalty, consideration or gratitude.

Nevertheless, he was eminently gifted. His Gide and Tchaikovsky
are very good books, and his *Vulcan*, except for the parts that he *could*
have done better, is perhaps the best of the refugee novels. One need
only consider his most successful works to see that his death is a great
loss. A good deal of injustice was done him, even in death. I can honestly
say that I always praised and encouraged him.

It has been costing me an absurd amount of trouble and torment to
write a lecture for Germany. And my ill humour is increased by my
regret that you and I have been unable to coordinate our travel plans.

We could have had such a pleasant meeting in Sils or somewhere else near here. Well, until next year.

    Yours ever,
      Thomas Mann

See LETTER SIXTY-SEVEN *below*.

LETTER
SIXTY-SEVEN

FROM HERMANN HESSE TO THOMAS MANN ON
THE DEATH OF THOMAS MANN'S BROTHER,
HEINRICH MANN.
17 MARCH 1950.

Dear Herr Thomas Mann,
With deep sympathy I have read the news of your brother's death. Of
all the strange and ambivalent things that old age brings us, the loss of
our intimates, especially the companions of our youth, is perhaps the
strangest. As little by little they all vanish away, so that in the end we
have more friends and intimates in the 'beyond' than here below, we
become curious about this beyond and lose the dread of it we had when
they walled us around more securely.

But with all our losses and all the loosening of our roots, we don't
put aside our egoism. And so, at the news of this death, after I had taken
it in and accustomed myself to it, my second and strongest thought was
of you, and the hope that this leavetaking may not make the thought of
your own leavetaking too easy for you, comes quite spontaneously and
selfishly to my heart and lips.

Yes, I fervently hope that your light may long continue to shine. It
gives me strength to know you are still there and accessible.

With warm regards from us both to you both.
Cordially,
H. Hesse

*Hermann Hesse (1877–1962), though born in Germany, spent most of his life
as a Swiss citizen. His father had been a missionary in India, and Hesse was
greatly influenced by his parents' religious outlook.*

He was a prolific writer, a pacifist and a humanitarian. In spite of persistent attacks from Germany and having his books black-listed there, he retained his faith in the fundamental purity of mankind.

He wrote short stories, novels and poetry, and received innumerable honours including the Nobel Prize for Literature in 1946.

One can well believe that in writing LETTER SIXTY-FIVE *Hesse had in mind the loss of his youngest son and of his first wife.*

Thomas Mann (1875–1955) was born at Lubeck to a family of grain merchants. At 18, after his father's death, he moved to Munich, where he worked in an insurance office and attended lectures at the University. He then went to Rome, began work on the novel Buddenbrooks *and this was published in 1901.*

His short stories had already attracted attention. He returned to Munich and joined the staff of a satirical journal Simplicissimus. *Publication of* Der Zauberberg, The Magic Mountain, *in 1924 confirmed his international reputation. In 1929 Mann was awarded the Nobel Prize for Literature.*

During the First World War Mann had published political essays in support of the German imperialist cause, but subsequently he became a firm supporter of social democracy. In 1933 he left Germany and eventually settled in the U.S.A. In 1947 his Doktor Faustus *was influenced greatly by what he saw as Germany's tragic destiny under Hitler. Mann spent the last two years of his life in Switzerland.*

From André Gide and the Crisis of Modern Thought, *by Klaus Mann, New York, 1943 –* LETTER SIXTY-FIVE. The Hesse-Mann Letters: The Correspondence of Hermann Hesse and Thomas Mann 1910–55, *edited* by Anni Carlsson and Volker Michels, London, n.d. – LETTERS SIXTY-SIX *and* SIXTY-SEVEN.

LETTER SIXTY-EIGHT

FROM SIR SAMUEL HOARE TO MRS NEVILLE
CHAMBERLAIN ON THE DEATH OF HER HUSBAND.
11 NOVEMBER 1940.

I cannot say with what sorrow I have heard the tragic news of Neville's death. I can only hope that he was spared suffering at the end. I am sure that he died as he lived, courageous, resolute and single-minded. Never did anyone more devotedly serve his country. Of all the public men that I have ever known, he was the most disinterested – and he was also the most modest. There was nothing artificial or insincere about him. These great qualities will be more and more appreciated. So also will his record of service at the Ministry of Health and the Treasury. Most of all will the world come to realise more clearly than is possible amidst the clouds of war his work for peace. Having been with him through the critical days of Munich I am more than ever conscious of the value of his efforts. He was right to make the attempt to save the world from a great catastrophe and history will give this verdict. But to-day I am not thinking so much of public affairs as of your great personal sorrow. For never were two closer together than Neville and you. You and he went hand in hand through all those difficult days and now that you are parted, I cannot bear to think of your sorrow. I can only say that if the loving sympathy of innumerable friends is a help to you you have it in the fullest measure. I wish indeed that I were at home to give you ours.

Sir Samuel Hoare (1880–1959) was a Conservative statesman, and in 1944 he became Lord Templewood. From 1922–9 he was the Air Secretary and he did much to improve the strength and effectiveness of the Royal Air Force. In 1938 he was one of the most influential supporters of the Munich Pact.

Neville Chamberlain will always occupy an unenviable place in history, and there can be precious few British Prime Ministers who showed quite such an incapacity to understand what was going on around them.

From The Life of Neville Chamberlain, *by Sir Keith Feiling, London,* 1970.

LETTER
SIXTY-NINE

VIRGINIA WOOLF TO MRS JACQUES RAVERAT
ON THE DEATH OF HER HUSBAND, JACQUES.
11 MARCH 1925.

Dearest Gwen,

Your and Jacques' letter came yesterday, and I go about thinking of you both in starts and almost constantly underneath everything, and I don't know what to say. The thing that comes over and over is the strange wish I have to go on telling Jacques things. This is for Jacques, I say to myself; I want to write to him about happiness, about Rupert [Brooke], and love. It had become to me a sort of private life, and I believe I told him more than anyone, except Leonard; I become mystical as I grow older and f(e' an alliance with you and Jacques which is eternal, not interrupted or hurt by never meeting. Then of course, I have now for you – how can I put it? – I mean the feeling that one must reverence? – is that the word – feel shy of, so tremendous an experience; for I cannot conceive what you have suffered. It seems to me that if we met, one would have to chatter about every sort of little trifle, because there is nothing to be said.

And then being, as you know, so fundamentally an optimist, I want to make you enjoy life. Forgive me, for writing what comes into my head. I think I feel that I would give a great deal to share with you the daily happiness. But you know that if there is anything I could ever give you, I would give it, but perhaps the only thing to give is to be oneself with people. One could say anything to Jacques. And that will always be the same with you and me. But oh, dearest Gwen to think of you is making me cry – why should you and Jacques have had to go through this? As I told him, it is your love and that has forever been love to me – all those years ago, when you used to come to Fitzroy Square, I was so angry and you were so furious, and Jacques wrote me a sensible manly letter, which I answered, sitting at my table in the window. Perhaps I was frightfully jealous of you both, being at war with the whole world at the moment. Still, the vision has become to me a source of wonder – the vision of your face; which if I were painting I should cover, with flames, and put you on a hill top. Then I don't think you would believe how it moves me that you and Jacques should have been reading Mrs Dalloway, and liking it. I'm awfully vain I know; and I was on pins and needles about sending it to Jacques; and now I feel exquisitely relieved; not flattered: but one does want that side of one to be acceptable – I was going to have written to Jacques about his children and about my having none – I mean, these efforts of mine to communicate with people are partly childlessness, and the horror that sometimes overcomes me.

There is very little use in writing this. One feels so ignorant, so trivial, and like a child, just teasing you. But it is only that one keeps thinking of you, with a sort of reverence, and of that adorable man, whom I loved.

Yours,
V.W.

Virginia Woolf (1882–1941) was a writer and critic and prominent member of the coterie known as 'The Bloomsbury Circle.'

Her sense of humour often led her into being cruel and hard, and she was ever wary of sentiment for fear of sentimentality. She was certainly one of the most original and outstanding writers of the twentieth century. Her elegant prose, one imagines, will be read as long as books are read. Like so many geniuses she was excessively vulnerable and prepared to drive herself into a frenzy of obsessive concentration for the sake of her work. She was frequently neurotic to the point of insanity and finally brave to the point of suicide.

Gwen Raverat (1885–1957) was an artist and writer and the daughter of Sir George Darwen, her mother was American. She married Jacques Raverat, a Frenchman, whom she met while they were both studying at the Slade School of Art. In 1947 she wrote a delightful book of childhood reminiscences called Period Piece. *In the last sentence of that book she writes: 'Oh dear, oh dear, how horrid it was being young, and how nice it is being old and not having to mind what people think!'*

Jacques Raverat was a painter and writer whose promising career was cut short by disseminated sclerosis.

From A Change of Perspective – The Letters of Virginia Woolf, *edited by Nigel Nicolson, London, 1977.*

LETTER SEVENTY

FROM C. RAJAGOPALACHARI TO THE SON OF
BHALUBHAI DESAI ON THE DEATH OF HIS FATHER.
30 MAY 1946.

If I repeat what others have said before it is because the truth is old, the
occasion is common and the wisdom is ancient. Why should we grieve?
Do we grieve for ourselves or for the departed? If for ourselves, we
should overcome it as soon as possible. If for the departed, it is unneces-
sary. He is gone, happily saved and received into the lap of the great all-
merciful mother. He has rejoined his true home, and that is why the
flowers bloom and the coconut trees bear fruit joyfully though silently.
The common mother of us all is not unkind, or forgetful or callous.
You too must soothe and cheer up one another and bravely learn to be
happy. I can see without your saying it the desolation – the dreadful
desolation. But let us learn to bear it – discover ways to dispel it – that
alone would cheer up the departed spirit who is watching over you
even now and waiting to see you happy, not to see you continue in
grief.

*C. Rajagopalachari (born in 1883) was India's last Governor-General, suc-
ceeding Lord Mountbatten, 1948–50. He was a long-time friend of Mahatma
Ghandi.*
    From The Political Career of C. Rajagopalachari – 1937–54: A
Moralist in Politics, *by A. R. H. Copley, Delhi, 1978.*

LETTER SEVENTY-ONE

D. H. LAWRENCE TO JOHN MIDDLETON MURRY
ON THE DEATH OF MURRY'S WIFE, KATHERINE
MANSFIELD.
NEW MEXICO, 2 FEBRUARY 1923.

Dear Jack,
I got your note just now, via Kot, about Katherine. Yes, it is something
gone out of our lives – we thought of her, I can tell you, at Wellington.
Did Ottoline ever send on the card to Katherine I posted from there for
her? Yes, I always knew a bond in my heart. Feel a fear where the bond
is broken now. Feel as if old moorings were breaking all. What is going
to happen to us all? Perhaps it is good for Katherine not to have to see the
next phase. We will unite up again when I come to England. It has been
a savage enough pilgrimage these last few years. Perhaps K. has taken
the only way for her. We keep faith – I always feel death only streng-
thens that, the faith between those who have it.

Still, it makes me afraid. As if worse were coming. I feel like the
Sicilians. They always cry for help from their dead – we shall have to
cry to ours: we do cry.

I wrote to you to Adelphi Terrace the day after I got your letter, and
asked Seltzer to send you *Fantasia of the Unconscious*. I wanted Katherine
to read it.

She'll know though. The dead don't die – they look on and help.

But in America one feels as if *everything* would die, and that is terrible.
I wish it needn't have all been as it has been: I do wish it.
     D.H.L.

D. H. Lawrence (1885–1930) was the most noted novelist and writer of his generation. Aldous Huxley has described him as a 'mystical materialist,' and Lawrence's letter above may well be seen as an example of that.

Katherine Mansfield was a short story writer and critic and her husband, John Middleton Murry, subsequently wrote a biography of her.

From The Letters of D. H. Lawrence, *edited by Aldous Huxley, London,* 1932.

LETTER SEVENTY-TWO

EDITH SITWELL TO MRS OWEN ON THE DEATH OF
HER SON, THE POET WILFRED OWEN.
LONDON, 3 OCTOBER 1919.

Dear Mrs Owen,
I have delayed writing this very impertinent letter in fear it should never
reach you owing to the strike; but there seems no hope of a settlement
for the moment, and I can delay it no longer.

Thank you so much for your letter; it was so very kind. I am distressed to hear you are in ill health. I know it is just then that those terrible longings creep in and tear you when you have no defence. There
is nothing to say to a woman who has lost what you have lost. But oh
what reason you have to be proud. And the day will come, dear Mrs
Owen, when you will hear your boy spoken of as the greatest poet this
war has produced. I think it must have been so wonderful for your son
to have such a mother. Your sympathy for his work must have meant
so much.

See further LETTER SEVENTY-FIVE.

LETTER SEVENTY-THREE

A FURTHER LETTER FROM EDITH SITWELL TO
MRS OWEN ON THE ANNIVERSARY OF THE
DEATH OF HER SON.
LONDON, 3 NOVEMBER 1919.

My dear Mrs Owen,
All my thoughts are with you today, and will be tomorrow increasingly. If only one could express what one feels, ever. My heart aches for you. I am dumb when I think what – not only you, his Mother, but we all have lost. I shall keep the 4 November [the day Wilfred Owen died] always as long as I live, as a day of mourning.

I know you are broken hearted, but oh, you are just the mother for such a son.

Tomorrow, his first poems in book form will be with you – the immortality of his great soul. What a wonderful moment it will be for you, though an agony too.

I cannot write more, because words are so little; before the face of your loss and your grief. They sound too cold.

I shall write in a few days' time. God bless you.

All my reverence and all my thoughts.
     Yours ever,
     Edith Sitwell

See LETTER SEVENTY-FIVE.

LETTER
SEVENTY-FOUR

EDITH SITWELL TO DR DOROTHEA WALPOLE ON
THE DEATH OF HER BROTHER.
RENISHAW HALL, 1 JULY 1941.

Dear Dr Walpole,
I did not write at first because I knew you would be overwhelmed with
letters, but I have felt for you so very deeply in your great sorrow and
terrible loss!

How much we all miss him – My brother Osbert and I talk of this
every day. We are only three – my two brothers and myself – of the
many many people to whom he has shown endless kindness, practical
sympathy and help – and such a wide and generous understanding of
motives, of aims, pioneer work, of everything that came under his eyes!
There can never have been a broader outlook, and all this in addition to
his own fine work. – How did he ever find time to do that work and all
those kindnesses? Osbert showed me your letter. I can understand what
a brother he must have been knowing the person he was.

I remember so well the time, many years ago, when Hugh and I were
both on the Committee that was going to choose a present for Thomas
Hardy on his 80th birthday – all the givers and signatories had to be
under a certain age – But Hugh said suddenly: 'We must ask May
Sinclair'. 'Oh', said somebody, 'she is much over the age limit'. 'I don't
care', said Hugh, 'She must be asked, it will hurt her dreadfully from
every point of view if she is not'.

Only a small thing, perhaps, but so typical of that delicate feeling for
others, that warm kindliness.

We have been more angry – all more angry – than you can know
over the mean, petty, envious notice in *The Times* and that man Pollock.

He is disgraced for ever by having written such a letter. We feel terribly about this pain having been added to what you are bearing in grief, and the dreadful suddenness of that grief.

In what contrast is that meanness to the noble tributes of T. S. Eliot, Sir Kenneth Clark and J. B. Priestley. Those will remain. The other things will go where all dirty things go.

You will not dream please of answering this letter – I just had to try and express how much I feel for you and for Hugh's brother in your grief – and to tell you how much we shall miss him.

Believe me, the deepest sympathy – Yours sincerely,
   Edith Sitwell

See below LETTER SEVENTY-FIVE.

LETTER
SEVENTY-FIVE

EDITH SITWELL TO MARY CAMPBELL AFTER THE
DEATH OF HER SON ROY CAMPBELL.
CASTELLO DI MONTEGUITONI, 23 SEPTEMBER
1957.

My dear Mary,
My thoughts have been with you all this time, in your great grief,
desolation and loneliness.

The reason I have not written before is because ever since the early
summer, griefs and disasters have been heaped on my head – to such a
degree that I wondered sometimes, if it was possible. The only thing to
do, at such a time, is to be silent to those who are suffering more deeply
than oneself – not to heap one's sorrows and troubles into their greater
ones, which is the height of selfishness. But now I realise that I must be
taught some lesson.

How are you, my dear Godmother? – I mean in your health? How
much I long to see you. And how deeply sad I am just to have missed
Anna – to whom my love – when she came to London.

The Sunday Times has promised me that I shall review Roy's poems
immediately they come out . . . I still cannot believe the dreadful thing
that has happened has. Dear Mary, my deep love to you and all my
thoughts.
Edith.

Osbert sends his love.

*Edith Sitwell (1887–1964) is one of the recent English poets better known in
her day for what she was than for what she wrote. An aristocrat by birth, she
had an instinctive feeling for eccentricity and delighted in teasing the public,*

who were therefore inclined to misinterpret the depth of feeling which lay behind her fantastic imagery and playful juggling with rhythms and verbal sounds. A small talent nonetheless.

Austere in appearance, with features that seemed to demand the laurel wreath, she was nevertheless kindly and generous to those who needed her help or to aspiring writers who excited her interest.

Wilfred Owen (1893–1918) is in many ways the most accomplished of the 'War Poets.' Edith Sitwell tells how the holographs of some of his poems were almost indecipherable because of the mud from the trenches where they were written. In a letter to Siegfried Sassoon Owen wrote: 'I don't want to write anything to which a soldier would say non compris.'

Hugh Walpole (1884–1941) was a tremendously popular and proliferate novelist in his day but he is little read now.

Roy Campbell (1901–57) was brought up in Rhodesia and Dame Edith in her autobiography describes him as one of the very great poets of our time.

From Edith Sitwell: Selected Letters, edited by John Lehmann and Derek Parker, London, 1970.

LETTER
SEVENTY-SIX

T. E. LAWRENCE TO MRS THOMAS HARDY ON
THE DEATH OF HER HUSBAND.
KARACHI, 15 JANUARY 1928.

Dear Mrs Hardy,
This is a Sunday, and an hour ago I was in my bed, listening to Beethoven's last quartet; when one of my fellows came in and said that Thomas Hardy is dead. We finished the quartet, because all at once it felt like him; and now I am faced with writing something for you to receive three weeks too late.

I was waiting for it, almost. After your letter came at Christmas I wanted to reply, but a paragraph in the papers said that he was ill. Then I held my breath. knowing the tenuous balance of his life, which one cold wind would finish. For years he has been transparent with frailty. You living with him, grew too used to it, perhaps, to notice it. It was only you who kept him alive all these years: you to whom I, amongst so many others, owed the privilege of having known him.

And now, when I should grieve for him and for you, almost it feels like a triumph. That day we reached Damascus, I cried, against all my control, for the triumphant thing achieved at last, fitly; and so the passing of Thomas Hardy touches me. He had finished and was so full a man. Each time I left Max Gate, having seen that, I used to blame myself for intruding upon a presence which had done with things like me and mine. I would half-determine not to trouble his peace again. But, as you know, I always came back the next chance I had. I think I'd have tried to come even if you had not been good to me: while you were very good; and Thomas Hardy.

So actually in his death I find myself thinking more of you. I am well off, having known him; you have given up so much of your own life and richness to a service of self-sacrifice. I think it is good for the general that one should do for the others what you have done for us all; but it is hard for you, who cannot see as clearly as we can how gloriously you succeeded, and be sure how worth while it was. T. H. was infinitely bigger than the man who died three days back – and you were one of the architects. In the years since *The Dynasts* the Hardy of stress has faded, and Thomas Hardy took his unchallenged – unchallengeable – place. Though, as once I told you, after a year of adulation the pack will run over where he stood crying 'There is no Thomas Hardy and never was'. A generation will pass before the sky will be perfectly clear of clouds for his shining. However, what's a generation to a sun! He is secure. How little that word meant to him!

This is not the letter I'd like to write. You saw though how I looked on him, and guessed, perhaps, how I'd have tried to think of him, if my thinking had had the compass to contain his image.

Oh, you will be miserably troubled now, with jackal things that don't matter: you, who have helped so many people and whom, therefore, no one can help. I am so sorry.

T. E. Lawrence

T. E. Lawrence (1888–1935), more popularly known as 'Lawrence of Arabia', fought with the Arabs in their revolt against Turkish domination during the First World War. He was a man of complex psychological motives and the hero worship and publicity which he attempted to 'escape' were largely of his own making. He was obsessed with speed and danger and died as a result of a motor-cycle crash.

Thomas Hardy (1840–1928), the novelist, and Lawrence became friends when Lawrence was serving with the Tank Corps and was stationed near Hardy's home, outside Dorchester.

From The Letters of T. E. Lawrence, *edited by David Garnett, London, 1938.*

LETTER
SEVENTY-SEVEN

BORIS PASTERNAK TO T. G. YASHVILI ON THE
DEATH OF HER HUSBAND.
28 AUGUST 1937.

My dear poor Tamara Georgiyevna,
What's all this? For a month I lived as though nothing had been happening and I knew nothing. I have known about it for about two weeks,
and all the time I go on writing to you, writing and tearing it up. My
existence no longer has any value, I am myself in need of comforting
and I do not know what to say to you that would not strike you as
idealistic verbiage and high-falutin pharisaism.

When I was told about it the first time, I did not believe it. It was
confirmed to me in town on the seventeenth. The shades and half
shades fell away. The news gripped me by the throat, I was in its power
and still am. Not everything that I experienced under the impact of that
terrible fact is irremediable and death – dealing – not everything.

When again and again I come to the realisation that never again shall
I see that wonderful face, with its high, inspired forehead and laughing
eyes and never hear the voice whose very sound was fascinating from its
overflow of ideas, I burst into tears, I toss about in anguish and can find
no place for myself. With thousands of well remembered details my
memory shows him to me in all the changes of the situations we have
been through together; in the streets of several towns, at excursions to
the sea and the mountains, at your home and at my home, on our latest
journeys, when presiding at conferences and on rostrums. The memory
wounds and drives the pain of bereavement to a point of insanity, flies
in my face with reproach. What have I done to be punished by an
eternity of this parting.

But it happened on the first day, the 17th, that its irreversibility cleansed me and brought me down to elementary facts which cannot be disputed, as in childhood, when after crying yourself into a torpor you suddenly want to eat and sleep from sheer fatigue. That blow was so powerful that it flung me far away from everything urban, from everything that is loud, not by right, not from necessity complicated, hysterically indifferent, eloquently empty. 'What nonsense', I said to myself again and again. Paolo? The Paolo I knew so well that I did not even care to analyse how I loved him – Paolo – the name of my delight, and everything that an average man A or an average man B might communicate to me with a serious air, men who will be forgotten in a moment, 'This', I thought, 'is for the future'. Everyone has to die anyway, and, moreover, in some kind of definite surroundings. So they will say: this life, preserved by posterity, came to an end in the summer of 1937, and they add the authentic facts of the time in question: the topics that occupied the minds of the public, the names of the papers, the names of acquaintances. In exactly the same way as in reference to some other age one would talk of wigs and jabots or, further back in time, of hunts with falcons.

So I carried this from town and got off at our station of Perdelkino. I knew that when I opened my mouth on the veranda to tell this to Zina, my voice would break and everything would be repeated afresh. But for the time being, on the way home, I gave myself up more and more, without relapsing, to the purifying force of grief, and how far did it take me!

I would have liked to have a bathe. The day was drawing to a close. On the bank, in the shady ravine, when after lying down comfortably I gradually recovered from the agitations of my journey, I suddenly began to catch here and there the features of some kind of marvellous likeness to the deceased. It was all inexpressably wonderful and terribly reminiscent of him. I saw bits and pieces of his spirit and style: his grass and water, his autumnal setting sun, his stillness, rawness and secretiveness. So, indeed, might he have said how they were burning and hiding, winking at each other and dying out. The sunset seemed to imitate him or reproduce him in memory.

I began thinking of him somehow in a new way. I always admired his talent, his unsurpassable flair for the picturesque, rare not only in Georgian literature, not only in the whole of our modern literature, but precious at any and every time. He always astonished me. People have letters which show how highly I thought of him. But it was for the first time that I began thinking of him quite apart from what I felt for him. Just as one moves away from something very, very big, his absolute outlines began to take shape only at the fateful distance of his loss. What he was away from us, away from me, Titian and Gogla, what he was not only apart from our admiration of him and our desire to see him victorious, but, on the contrary, in defiance of our love, what he was himself, with the water and the woods and God and the future.

Need I expatiate on that? About him who in the future will be Georgian Mayakovsky, on whose models the future young literature, if it is destined to develop, will emulate and study. But that side of immortality never troubled me. What surprises me is something else, however difficult it may be to express it; how much of him there remains in what he touched and what he named; in the hours of the day, in the flowers and animals, in the verdure of the woods, in the autumn sky. We lived and did not know the power he wielded among us, the authority that he still retains.

Dear Tamara Georgiyevna, forgive me. One must not write like that, one must not to you. Poetry and bad poetry at that, is out of place here. But I'll send off what I have written all the same, or when else shall I at last say the only thing that matters, that draws me so powerfully to you and to the unimaginably precious Medea. That is not complicated and you know it without me. Though you have no lack of friends and never will have, number me among them. However difficult my existence has become of late, nothing will be impossible for me as far as you are concerned. How much I should have liked to see you! I am asking Titian and Nina to embrace you for me, to be together with you and weep with you. And once more forgive me for this silly, feeble letter. But, then, I know nothing, even now. Would you write to me sometime afterward when you feel able to do so?

All yours,
B.P.

Boris Pasternak (1890–1960) was a writer and poet who achieved world-wide fame with his novel Dr Zhivago *for which he was awarded, but declined, the Nobel Prize for Literature in 1959.*

Pasternak was a victim of Soviet oppression and he will be remembered as one of the greatest of Russian writers since Chekov.

From Letters to Georgian Friends, *translated by David Magarshak, London, 1968.*

LETTER SEVENTY-EIGHT

ALDOUS HUXLEY TO MRS MARTHA SAXTON ON
THE DEATH OF HER HUSBAND.
6 JULY 1943.

My dear Martha,
I have been away from home and the news about Gene reached me only today. As I think about him now, I realise with surprise how few in all these years were the occasions on which I was with him, and how brief – and yet I always thought of him as one among the best of my friends. It was as though he possessed some quality stronger than absence and distance – an essential lovableness and reliability and warmth that continued to affect one, in spite of the obstacles interposed by space and time.

In a curious hardly analysable way Gene was for me, a living proof of the triumph of character over matter – physically almost always absent, and yet firmly present in my mind as a trusted friend, to whom I knew I could turn in any crisis without fear of disappointment.

And to you, dear Martha, what can I possibly say – There are no consolations that can be administered from without – only the mitigations of grief that come with time, and perhaps one's own tentative answers to the agonizing questions of life and death.

Ever yours affectionately,
Aldous H.

See LETTER EIGHTY.

LETTER
SEVENTY-NINE

ALDOUS HUXLEY TO MRS JEFFREY CORNER ON
THE DEATH OF HER HUSBAND (INCLUDED WITH
WHICH WAS THE NOTE HERE APPENDED FROM
LAURA HUXLEY, THE WIFE OF ALDOUS).
17 JUNE 1960.

My dear Jeff,
What can one say – there are no consolations. There is only the bearing
of the unbearable for the sake of the life – your own and the children's
that has to go on and be made the best of.

I never knew Doug well – but always felt, whenever I met him, a
renewal of the liking and respect that my first meeting had inspired.
One had a sense when one was with him that here was an intrinsically
good human being, decent, fair, kind, strong but never bumptious or
overbearing, with that blessed capacity for seeing himself with a humour-
ous eye which is a true manifestation of the Christian virtue of humility.
And now this dreadful senseless thing has happened – and you are left to
cope with the consequences – as I said there are no consolations; but
out of my own experience I can tell you certain things which may be of
some practical help. It is profoundly important to remember that, over
and above the grief and the loneliness and the near despair there will be
an organic reaction, closely resembling surgical shock. A bereavement
such as yours is an amputation, and like every other amputation it
produces a state of psychic and physical shock – a state which may last
for weeks or months. For so long as this state of shock persists the mind-
body requires appropriate supportive treatment in the form of adequate
rest, a good diet etc. The bereaved person's tendency is to resent this –
to feel that it is an ignoble kind of escape from the situation. But

neglecting the amputated organism will do nothing to spiritualise the bereavement. On the contrary it may physiologise it, transform it into sickness that leaves the sufferer no power to think with love about the past or act constructively in the present, and in relation to the children.

Yours affectionately
Aldous

My dear Jeff,
I would like to call you and see you, but maybe it is better if I let you call. Please do, soon. I think of you, and feel with you, intensely.

Until soon,
Laura

See LETTER EIGHTY.

LETTER EIGHTY

ALDOUS HUXLEY TO MRS MARGARET
KISKADDEN ON THE DEATH OF HER HUSBAND.
23 MAY 1962.

My dear Peggy,
Opening today's *New York Times*, I was distressed to read of the news of
Curtis's death. These vital threads that link the present to the past – how
many of them have already been broken, and how increasingly often as
one grows older, does one receive the news of yet another break! And
the questions keep multiplying. How are we related to what we were?
Who are we now and what were we then? And who were the others –
in our minds, in their minds, in the mind of omniscience? There are no
answers, of course – only the facts of living, changing, remembering
and at last dying.
    Affectionately,
     Aldous

Aldous Huxley (1894–1963) wrote many books and Brave New World *and*
Point Counter Point *are possibly the best known. He was a seeker who
consistently refused ever to be sure. He set great value on the individual's private vision and considered that 'the aim and purpose of life is the unitive knowledge of God.'*

    *Eugene Saxton was a writer and journalist who became Huxley's publisher.
They were great friends.*

    *Mrs Jeffrey Corner was the daughter of Huxley's friend, Mrs Betty
Wendel.*

    *Dr William Kiskadden, was a noted plastic surgeon, and he and his wife
were close to the Huxleys.*

    From Aldous Huxley – Letters, *edited by Grover Smith, London, 1969 –*
LETTERS SEVENTY-EIGHT, SEVENTY-NINE *and* EIGHTY.

LETTER EIGHTY-ONE

C. S. LEWIS TO HIS FATHER ON THE DEATH OF
W. T. KIRKPATRICK.
23 APRIL 1921.

I can of course appreciate your feelings about poor Kirk's funeral. Stripped of all wherewith belief and tradition have clothed it, death appears a little grimmer – a shade more chilly and loathsome – in the eyes of the most matter of fact. At the same time, while this is sad, it would have been not only sad but shocking to have pronounced over Kirk words that he did not believe and performed ceremonies which he himself would have denounced as meaningless. Yet, as you say, he is so stamped on one's mind, so often present in thought, that he makes his own acceptance and annihilation the more unthinkable. I have seen death fairly often and never yet been able to find it anything but extraordinary and rather incredible. The real person is so very real, so obviously living and different from what is left, that one cannot believe something has turned into nothing. It is not faith, is not reason – just a 'feeling' . . . .

See LETTER EIGHTY-FOUR *following.*

LETTER EIGHTY-TWO

C. S. LEWIS TO OWEN BARFIELD ON THE DEATH
OF CHARLES WILLIAMS.
  18 MAY 1945.

It has been a very odd experience. This, the first really severe loss I have
suffered has (a) given a corroboration to my belief in immortality such
as I never dreamed of – it is almost tangible now; (b) swept away all my
old feelings of mere horror and disgust at funerals, coffins, graves, etc. –
if need had been I think I could have handled *that* corpse with hardly any
unpleasant sensations; (c) greatly reduced my feeling about ghosts. I
think (but who knows?) that I should be, though afraid, more pleased
than afraid if his turned up . . . To put it in a nutshell, what the idea of
death has done to him is nothing to what he had done to the idea of
death. Hit it for six; yet it used to rank as a fast bowler!

See LETTER EIGHTY-FOUR.

LETTER EIGHTY-THREE

C. S. LEWIS TO A LADY ON THE DEATH OF
CHARLES WILLIAMS.
  20 MAY 1945.

I also have become acquainted with grief now through the death of my
great friend, Charles Williams, my friend of friends, the comforter of
all our little set, the most angelic man – the odd thing is that his death
had made my faith stronger than it was a week ago. And I find that all
that talk about 'feeling that he is closer to us than before' isn't just talk.
It's just what it does feel like – I can't put it into words. One seems at
moments to be living in a new world. Lots, lots of pain, but not a
particle of depression or resentment.

See LETTER EIGHTY-FOUR.

LETTER
EIGHTY-FOUR

C. S. LEWIS TO MISS VERA MATTHEWS ON THE
DEATH OF HER FATHER.
27 MARCH 1951.

I have just got your letters of the 22nd containing the sad news of your father's death. But, dear lady, I hope you and your mother are not really trying to pretend it didn't happen. It does happen, happens to all of us, and I have no patience with the high-minded people, who make out that it 'doesn't matter'. It matters a great deal, and very solemnly. And for those who are left, the pain is not the whole thing. I feel very strongly (and I am not alone in this) that some good comes from the dead to the living in the months or weeks after the death. I think I was much helped by my own father after his death; as if Our Lord welcomed the newly dead with the gift of some power to bless those they have left behind . . . Certainly they often seem just at that time to be very near us.

C. S. Lewis (1898–1963), a writer and critic, best known perhaps for The Screwtape Letters. *He was born in Ireland and sent to public school in England. Here he was so unhappy that his father removed him and sent him to W. T. Kirkpatrick at Great Bookham in Surrey to read for an Oxford Scholarship. He describes his days here in* Surprised by Joy. *At last he was stimulated to the full and Kirkpatrick understood him perfectly. In December 1916 he was elected to an open Scholarship at University College, Oxford.*

   Charles Williams was one of Lewis' greatest friends and like him was a member of the rather odd Inklings, a sort of literary Elks club that met every Thursday evening in C. S. Lewis' rooms in Magdalen College.

   From The Letters of C. S. Lewis, *edited by W. H. Lewis, London, 1966 –* LETTERS EIGHTY-ONE, EIGHTY-TWO, EIGHTY-THREE, and EIGHTY-FOUR.

LETTER
EIGHTY-FIVE

NANCY MITFORD TO HER COUSIN ANN HORNE
ON THE DEATH OF HER HUSBAND, DAVID HORNE.
HOSPITAL ROTHSCHILD, 7 APRIL 1970.

Darling Id,

I'm so distressed to hear of your loss – a great loss to a great many
people – such a particularly charming man. Oh dear, the sorrows there
are as life goes on it is hardly bearable – this last year seems to me to
have been particularly dire.

I'm here for examinations – have never been in hospital and I mustsay
it's rough work for somebody as spoilt as I am. All the other people are
100 times worse and much poorer than me, which might cheer me up
but somehow it doesn't!! Only a few more days – soon be over.

I do wish I ever saw you. It's nice that Decca is coming over for a long
visit. Why don't you come to Versailles with her – I would put her in an
hotel and you could stay with me. Think of it.

    Much love
    Nancy.

*Nancy Mitford (1904–73) was a novelist and historical biographer. At about
the time this letter was written Nancy Mitford's world was collapsing round
her. She had already been suffering for over a year from the cruel illness which
she was to die of three years later. One after the other friends died and her
health deteriorated to such an extent that it must have taken super-human
courage to exist. Her letters make sad but never dull reading. She seldom dis-
guised her suffering or her moments of self-pity – no false heroics, only the
jokes which for years had become an integral part of her personality now
served more than ever to entertain her friends and to keep her spirits up. The*

fact that she shared her feelings with her family and her friends highlighted her courage. Even in a condolence letter she is not afraid to mention her own trouble and rightly since this is always the greatest compliment any of us can give our friends.

In her books and her letters she showed herself to be an original witty and highly civilized individual.

Decca was a younger sister and famous in her right as the author of, amongst many other books, Hons and Rebels.

David Horne (1898–1970) was a leading stage and film actor in his day. He had been left for dead on a battlefield in the First World War but was nevertheless rescued and nursed back to health at King Edward VII's Hospital for Officers.

LETTER
EIGHTY-SIX

REX WHISTLER TO MRS BELLOC-LOWNDES ON
THE DEATH OF HER HUSBAND.
LONDON, 28 MARCH 1940.

Darling Mrs Lowndes,
I have just heard with great pain of your loss.

There is nothing that I can say – or probably anyone else – that could
alleviate your unhappiness, particularly as, with the person you so love,
must seem to have gone too all those long loving years of peaceful con-
tentment and delight. It is true, I think, that they only seem to have
gone, for that lovely store of golden years which you made together –
years of life well lived, full of delightful interests shared and lovely
pleasant things, is really as much with you now as say last month – last
year – anytime, for the triumph and delight of such a thing as you both
made of life is a cumulative one.

Any one day it has no more power than another, and yet the WHOLE
– whether yesterday or thirty years ago – being the Past, cannot be
affected by the Present.

But all that of course you know, and the pain in your heart is for the
Present and the Future without that companion who made life so
agreeable and lovely in the past. But in your unhappiness now I am
very sure you are nearer and more in touch than ever I shall be, with
the one unfailing source of comfort and strength to the Spirit.

I have often thought how curiously short lived and how small is the
quantity of happiness we are allowed at a time (the quality of happiness
is of course beyond measure). We seem to pass so rapidly from light
into shadow, and when in light again darkness seems invariably to
follow, so much too quickly.

And yet I suppose it is really the exquisite *taste* and *economy* of the Genius who draws our loves which makes life so infinitely lovely and moving, stirring and glorious. It is as though we presumed to stand by the side of a great painter imploring him not to use the dark tones and shadows, but only to put light and more light. How can we know what the great mind has already conceived the finished work to be?

My darling Mrs Lowndes, I feel deeply for you in your grief and for your dear sweet Elizabeth and Susan, I only hope you will believe this, and not think this foolish 'rigmarole' a duty letter. I keep you always in my heart as a VERY dear friend. On no account think of answering this.

Very affectionately always,
Rex Whistler.

Rex Whistler (1905–44) was an artist and one of the greatest losses suffered by British art during the Second World War. At a time when the prevailing trend was towards primitive and surrealist eccentricity Whistler went for a facile, elegant and witty sophistication. Hence his engaging Spirit of Brighton in the Pavilion there – his spiritual home. Better known perhaps are the murals in the Restaurant of the Tate Gallery, which were commissioned from him when he was twenty.

Mrs Belloc-Lowndes was a novelist and sister of Hilaire Belloc.

From My Life and Letters, *by Marie Belloc-Lowndes, London, 1971.*

LETTER EIGHTY-SEVEN

MARTYN SKINNER TO AILWYN BEST ON THE
DEATH OF HIS WIFE ELIZABETH BEST.
TAUNTON, 14 MARCH 1971.

My dear Ailwyn,

You will have had a very large number of letters; and I know that
Pauline has written a long one. But I feel I must let you know that I do
sympathise most deeply with you and the family – I can judge in a
small way what the shock must have been for you, by knowing what I
felt myself.

What a marvellous person she was – so lively and gay, full of the zest
of life and capacity for appreciation and enjoyment! And such a brave
and dauntless SPIRIT! All the same she wouldn't have taken well to an
invalid life, as you must have told yourself many times.

> Then with no fiery throbbing pain,
> No cold gradations of decay
> Death snapped at once the vital chain
> And freed her soul the nearest way.

A way for her, if it had to be; and in a way fitting; she surely wasn't
meant for the frustration and humiliations of illness and old age.

But only in a way, of course – for she had so much to give, especially
to her family with her capacity for affection and helpfulness and her
absorbing interest in her grand-children. You must all be feeling to its
full depth the meaning of bereavement – and how deep it can be. I have
experienced it myself and I can share in what you must be suffering.

I had a characteristically generous and appreciative letter from her
written I suppose shortly before she died; it will be a poignant but happy

and treasured possession. And what good-fortune it was – for us – that we were able to enjoy such a very happy week-end as that one was.

You will have many letters to cope with; please believe I really mean it when I say I don't expect an answer to this.

Yours ever,
Martyn.

Martyn Skinner (born 1906) is a poet and writer and the author of several books, including Letters to Malaya *and* The Return of Arthur. *In 1943 he was awarded the Hawthornden Prize and in 1947 the Heinemann Award.*

Ailwyn Best is an architect who works on the renovation of historic buildings and country houses. He is also an accomplished singer and composer.

LETTER
EIGHTY-EIGHT

FROM ORMEROD GREENWOOD TO ANN HORNE
ON THE DEATH OF HER HUSBAND.
EASTBOURNE, 20 MARCH 1970.

Dear Ann,
I am more touched than I can say that you wanted me to be at Golders
Green yesterday – I never felt that I knew David well, yet I loved and
admired him – and although it is so long since we met, he has been a
part of my life since I left Cambridge in 1931. I am sure, too, that we
need some kind of ceremony for the great occasions of life, if life is to
have any significance (this may sound odd for a Quaker – but I think
it is one of the functions of religion) and I fear we are losing our sense
of this, especially in our fear of death – the unmentionable thing, which
we ought to be able to accept. For the same reason I hate registry office
weddings and am sorry that our youngest daughter Liz will have one,
next month.

I do pray that you will find the strength you need to cope with everything that your bereavement brings, and that all that was best in David
will remain with you, not just to give you a sense of loss, but to comfort
and console you.

> Man was made for Joy or Woe,
> And when this we rightly know
> Through the world we safely go.
> Joy and Woe are woven fine
> A clothing for the Soul Divine.

Your friend
Ormerod.

Ormerod Greenwood (born 1907) is an actor, broadcaster, writer, and lecturer. He is an active member of the Society of Friends (Quakers).

David Horne was a Quaker too and Ormerod Greenwood took the Meeting for Worship at his funeral at Golders Green Crematorium.

LETTER
EIGHTY-NINE

FROM RUTH PLANT TO MISS E. EDMONDS ON THE
DEATH OF HER SISTER.
BUCKINGHAMSHIRE, 20 FEBRUARY 1976.

My dear Elgiva,
I feel I must send you this note to give you my loving sympathy in this
sudden departure of Esther for the next life, because it is so difficult to
say these things, when so many people are coming and going.

Also, as I think I did explain it seems rather bad taste to rush in with
one's personal convictions about survival, and try to foist them on someone else at such a time – but you asked about this, so I am writing this
note.

We have been awfully lucky in having some extraordinary proofs of
survival, and one can only pass on the facts to others, not the personal
experiences. Some people are helped by this . . .

I recall the time when Colette Yardly came to live here and was
amazed to recognise in my Mother's photo the lady with lovely white
hair who had visited her every night for some weeks, looking her up
and down, as if vetting her for something! This was *before* she had ever
heard of us from Petronella. We had been getting messages from
Mummie that she had found a much younger person to follow the two
old ladies as tenant in the flat and she would see that she was brought to
the house presently.

How typical of my Mother to want to be involved in choosing the
person who would come and live in my home and look after her beloved animals when I was out! It seems only logical to think therefore
that it was Mummie Colette saw as she said.

Then there was the time I met Father Jellicoe in a dream, after he died, and as he came towards me to greet me and as he put his arm out, I passed into such an extraordinary area of happiness, like coming out into warm sunshine after being under a tree. It was a kind of happiness I can't describe at all – because we don't have it here. It was devoid of fear and devoid of the feeling that it would fade or alter on a difficult day. I found myself saying 'Oh, I can't go back to the earth after this with all its fears and uncertainties'.

Then I realised that though we probably meet our dear ones in the After Life in sleep, we cannot bring the memory back because we still have to go on working for people on the earth.

Do excuse this note written at 1 am.

Love and sympathy,

Ruth Plant is the Regional Officer of the Churches' Fellowship for Psychic and Spiritual Studies and the author of Journey into Light *and* Nanny and I. *She was born in 1909, the daughter of an English clergyman.*

Colette Yardley is now the wife of the composer Doctor Edmund Rubbra.

Father Basil Jellicoe was a priest who founded the first privately-funded housing association in England, the St Pancras House Improvement Association. He died at the age of thirty-three.

LETTER NINETY

JOYCE GRENFELL TO LAVINIA DYER ON THE
DEATH OF HER HUSBAND REX.
CHELSEA, 1975.

Dear Lavinia,
Diana Lydon told me your tragic news and I write to send my thoughts
and my real sympathy. I think perhaps there is an affinity between those
who know what a good marriage is and my own . . . fills me with
compassion for you at this sad time. I don't know how you feel about it
but I am increasingly sure that life is spiritual and therefore continuous –
not in any spiritualistic way (material) but as the actual fact of our being,
and because I believe this I'm sure that prayer which says 'Death is an
horizon and our horizon is but the limitation of our view' is the truth.

We can *never* lose anything that is good never lose love or the memories of great happiness because they are *true*. I've come to the conclusion
that only the eternal is real! And that means qualities that one loves in
people – their humour, generosity, honour, kindness, gentleness etc.
are the reality: and can never die. They are the identity of the one one
loves.

I just felt I wanted to write to send you my thoughts and feeling and
affection.
    Yours,
      Joyce Grenfell.

*Joyce Grenfell (1910–79) was half American by birth – her mother was
Nancy Astor's sister – and she became one of England's most popular and loved
actresses and entertainers.*

    *She was a life-long Christian Scientist – like her aunt – and as can be seen
from this letter she had an exceedingly happy marriage.*

    A Memorial Service was held for her in Westminster Abbey.

LETTER
NINETY-ONE

ELIZABETH MYERS TO RUTH FORSTER ON THE
DEATH OF A FRIEND.
SHERBORNE, 13 AUGUST 1946.

Dear Ruth,
I am sorry you have had this sad experience and I hope that by now you
have been able to see things in the right perspective, realising that you
did all that could be done, and that neither you nor the patient's husband have *lost* your friend because she is dead. *People don't die unless we
let them.* No: I can't agree that death is cruel. For those who go *it is the
way to life*, the full splendid life for which the time here is only a
preparation.

The sadness about this girl's death is that she should have begged
'Don't let me die'. If only someone had shown her that death, so far
from being cruel, is an act of love rounding off our brief testing here,
she need not have gone in so much regret because she would have understood that she would not be separated from you and her husband. She is,
in fact, nearer to you now than in her hospital bed. Death is an enlarging
of the degrees of sensibility. We who are left are debarred from much
because of the limitations of sensibility imposed on us by our physical
frame-work. Your friend is not lost or gone and your love is not in vain.
Have faith and be comforted by her nearness.

I trust all will be well with you. We all have our work to do here,
Ruth, but we all belong *somewhere* else. Your friend is happy. Think of
it for her and be happy too.

Yours
Elizabeth.

Elizabeth Myers (1912–47) was a novelist, writer, and critic. At the age of twenty-five she was shattered to find that she had contracted tuberculosis and felt she could never endure all the suffering and restrictions that illness involves. However, she turned her tragedy to good account and after fifteen months at a stretch in hospital she said she had learnt how to think and be really and lastingly happy.

From The Letters of Elizabeth Myers, *Introduction by Littleton C. Powers, London, 1951.*

LETTER
NINETY-TWO

JESSICA MITFORD TO HER COUSIN MRS DAVID
HORNE (ANN FARRER) ON THE DEATH OF HER
HUSBAND.
A CABLE FROM OAKLAND, CALIFORNIA,
23 MARCH 1970.

Sister darling have just heard most terribly desperately sorry cannot
write because postal strike this brings all our love.

FOLLOWED BY A LETTER DATED 26 MARCH 1970.

Oh Sister, I was so *desperately* sad to hear. There's been a postal strike
this end, but Sonia sent me the thing from *The Times*, and somehow it
did arrive. But I couldn't write until now, no letters going out.

Cyst, what can I say. I know how *terrible* it is for you. I keep thinking
back to those delightful meals the three of us had at nearby restaurants
when I was in London, he was in all ways such an absolutely sweet
person, really very, very rare. In the last few years, when we've seen
more of each other, I felt I was really getting to know him and his
marvellous qualities of kindness and amusingness.

Sister, this is just to bring *all* my love.

Yr. *Sister.*

Give Clare a HUGE hug from me.

*Jessica Mitford (born in 1917) is the fifth of the Mitford sisters. She is known
as 'Decca' and she and Ann Farrer were much of an age and had been friends
almost from the cradle. They shared the enormous excitement of filmgoing
together when they were about twelve, hence their use of the American 1930s
term Sister (and Cyst). In fact they are cousins.*

Nancy, the eldest of the Mitfords – see LETTER EIGHTY-FIVE *– was the first to make her name as a writer, but Decca, though younger and starting later, has been no less successful. Her books include:* Hons and Rebels, The American Way of Death, *and* A Fine Old Conflict.
Decca lives in Oakland, California.

LETTER NINETY-THREE

CHRISTOPHER PROBST TO HIS MOTHER, AND TO HIS SISTER.
MUNICH, 22 FEBRUARY 1943.

I thank you for having given me life. When I really think it through it has been a single road to God. Do not grieve that I must now skip the last part of it. Soon I shall be closer to you than before. In the meantime I'll prepare a glorious reception for you all.

TO HIS SISTER.

I never knew that dying is so easy . . . I die without any feeling of hatred . . . never forget that life is nothing but a growing in love and a preparation for eternity.

Christopher Probst (died 1943) was one of the group of Munich students caught while dropping leaflets from a gallery into the main lobby of the University, calling upon German people to free their country from the criminal dictatorship that governed them, and demand peace.
   He wrote these letters on the day of his execution. His mother and sister were permitted to read his farewell letters in the presence of a Gestapo official, but the letters were not handed over to them. The excerpts were set down from memory shortly afterwards.
   From Dying We Live, *introduction by Trevor Huddleston, London, 1956.*

LETTER NINETY-FOUR

TO HIS INFANT SON JAN FROM A CZECH RESISTANCE WORKER EXECUTED IN MARCH 1944. WRITTEN TO HIS WIFE.

Teach our son Jan. And above all, teach him courage. Let him have an immediate approach to everything about him. Teach him to enjoy victory over hatred and envy. It needs courage to have a pure heart. He should excel in the art of tolerance – thus will he find faith in himself and God. Only thus will he carry within him strength to understand and forgive.

The old world lacked such courage; it was accustomed to fear. The present day seeks security by fighting against such fear. We bring a noble inheritance to the future – the courage that is born of struggle, in the midst of which emerges slowly a faith in the new and true mission of humanity. But the discovery that what is lacking is imaginative power, without which men cannot penetrate into the feelings of others, that is the discovery of the future, the discovery of Jan – yes, of your coming day, my son. . . .

My dear, at the beginning of your life I expressed the desire, in the presence of the Almighty, that you obtain true education of the spirit – not merely knowledge – that you may become a man pure as crystal, defending fearlessly everything that he thinks good and true, if necessary against all. . . . And further, pay more attention to men than things, and remember that Divine wisdom is always better than human.

This letter is an abbreviated version of one published in The Friend *just after the last war, on 9 August 1946. It was sent to the editor by Sylvia Stahlova, a letter of condolence from a father (before he was executed by the Nazis) to his infant son Jan, in March 1944. The man was associated with the Prague Friends (Quakers).*

From The Friend *(London), 9 August 1946.*

ACKNOWLEDGE-MENTS

WE WOULD like to thank the following for their help to us in compiling this anthology: Hildburg Braun for her translation of Goethe's letter to Zelter; Elizabeth Hamilton-Jones for her translation of the letters of Madame de Sévigné and Lamartime; R. E. C. Swann for his help with some of the notes; Ann Jones, Mary Mayfield, and Eva Walker for help with the typing; Anthony Copley; Joan Bligh; William Fortescue; Ailwyn Best; Lavinia Dyer; Anne Horne; Elgiva Edmonds; Guy Harding; and the staffs of Buckingham Library, Beaconsfield Library, the British Library, Guildhall Library, the Bodleian Library, and the Guildhall Library.

We would like to thank our husbands for their help and encouragement.

If copyright material has been (unwittingly) infringed within this book the editors and publishers will be pleased to hear from anyone with proof of ownership.

Thanks are due to the following for permission to reproduce copyright works: LETTER FIVE – Shepheard-Walwyn (Publishers) Ltd, from *The Ficino Letters;* LETTER SIXTEEN – Geoffrey Purefoy Esq; LETTERS THIRTY-FIVE, THIRTY-SIX and THIRTY-SEVEN – John Murray (Publishers) Ltd, from *Byron's Letters and Journals*, volume 2, edited by Leslie A. Marchand; LETTER FIFTY-TWO – The Christian Science Board of Directors, 1913, and renewed 1941; LETTER FIFTY-SIX – The Trustees of the late Mrs Patrick Campbell; LETTER FIFTY-SEVEN – Longman Group Ltd, from *Grey of Fallodon* by G. M. Trevelyan; LETTERS SIXTY-ONE, SIXTY-TWO, and SIXTY-THREE – A. R. Mowbray and Company Ltd, from *The Life and Letters of Father Andrew SDC*, edited by Kathleen E. Burne, and *The Spiritual Letters of Father Hughson;* LETTER SIXTY-FIVE – Octagon Press (New York), from *Andrè Gide*

INDEX OF WRITERS

INDEXED BY LETTER NUMBERS

INDEX OF RECIPIENTS

INDEXED BY LETTER NUMBERS